Tea Cozies 4

Tea Cozies 4

THE GUILD OF MASTER CRAFTSMAN

PUBLICATIONS

First published 2013 by
Guild of Master Craftsman Publications Ltd
Castle Place, 166 High Street
Lewes, East Sussex BN7 1XU

Copyright in the Work © GMC Publications Ltd, 2013

ISBN: 978-1-86108-966-3

A catalogue record for this book is available from
the British Library.

Publisher: Jonathan Bailey
Production Manager: Jim Bulley
Managing Editor: Gerrie Purcell
Project Editors: Cath Senker and Sara Harper
Managing Art Editor: Gilda Pacitti
Designer: Ginny Zeal
Photographer: Laurel Gilfoyle

Set in Gill Sans
Colour origination by GMC Reprographics
Printed and bound in China

Note
If you cannot find the yarn specified, you can use
a substitute of the same weight. Contact your yarn
supplier for advice.

Why do we love tea cozies?

SHARING A POT OF TEA IS A GESTURE OF FRIENDSHIP.
It is an opportunity to share exciting news or to have a reviving brew
at the end of the day, and it is the ideal way to welcome a visitor. Yet, as
we rush about, we often have time only to dunk a teabag into a mug and
gulp down a few mouthfuls before hurrying out of the door. The teapot is
left forlorn, gathering dust at the back of the cupboard.

We think it's time to dust off the teapot, dress it up with a stylish cozy
and use it for its intended purpose. Why not invite your friends round for
a really delicious treat? What could be better than enjoying a lavish spread
of cakes alongside the iconic centrepiece: a steaming-hot teapot specially
dressed for the occasion?

Our fourth tea-cozy title contains 30 innovative knitting and crochet designs
from experienced yarn-craft authors and the winners of our recent tea-cozy
knitting competition. They are all designed to fit an average six-cup teapot. You're
sure to have fun making your tea cozies and to enjoy them for years to come.

Contents

25

26

27

28

29

30

The heart on this design is worked separately and attached using blanket stitch, so there is no need for complicated colour changes. The yarn is held double so the resulting fabric is thick and fast to knit.

With love

Materials

Patons Fairytale Colour 4 Me DK, 100% wool
(98yds/90m per 50g ball)
2 × 50g balls in 04962 Pale Pink (A)
Oddment of deep pink DK yarn for the heart (B)
Pair of 4mm (UK8:US6) knitting needles
Pair of 5mm (UK6:US8) knitting needles
Stitch holder or spare needle
Tiny amount of washable polyester toy stuffing
Dressmaking pins
Tapestry needle

Tension

12 sts and 18 rows to 4in (10cm) in width over st st using 5mm needles and the yarn held double. Use larger or smaller needles if necessary to obtain the correct tension.

Sides

Side 1

Using 5mm needles and two strands of yarn A, cast on 28 sts and work 4 rows in g st.

Next row: Inc1, k across row until last st, inc1 (30 sts).

Work a further 7 rows in g st.

Next row: Knit across.

Next row: K2, p to last 2 sts, k2.

Rep last 2 rows eight times. Work should measure 5in (12.5cm). Adjust length here if necessary.

Break off yarn and set stitches aside on a stitch holder or spare needle.

Side 2

Work as for side 1, but do not break off yarn.

Join sides

Knit across 30 sts of side 1, then knit across 30 sts of side 2 (60 sts).

Next row: Purl all sts.

Next row: (K4, skpo) to end (50 sts).

Next row: Purl.

Next row: (K3, skpo) to end (40 sts).

Next row: Purl.

Next row: (K2, skpo) to end (30 sts).

Next row: Purl all sts.

Next row: (K1, skpo) to end (20 sts).

Next row: Purl.

Next row: (Skpo) to end (10 sts).

Work 6 rows of st st on these 10 sts for spike.

Next row: (Skpo) to end (5 sts).

Next row: Purl.

Break off yarn, thread end through stitches and fasten off securely, leaving a long end for sewing up.

Heart motif

Using 4mm needles and oddment of
yarn B, cast on 2 sts.

Row 1: Inc in first st, k1 (3 sts).

Row 2: Inc in first st, k2 (4 sts).

Row 3: Inc in first st, k3 (5 sts).

Cont in this way until there are 14 sts
on needle.

Work 8 rows in g st.

Next row: K2tog, k to last 2 sts, k2tog
(12 sts).

Next row: Knit.

Next row: K2tog, k2, k2tog. Turn
work, leaving last 6 sts on a stitch
holder or spare length of yarn.

Next row: K4.

Next row: K2tog, k2.

Next row: K2tog, k1.

Cast off last 2 sts. Rejoin yarn to 6 sts
set aside and complete in same way.

Making up

Join the garter-stitch sections at the
bottom side edges of the cozy. Join the
top side edges of the cozy to the start
of the two-stitch garter-stitch border.
Using the point of a knitting needle,
insert a small amount of stuffing into
the spike.

Catch the stitch in place from the
inside, ensuring that no stitches show
on the right side. Pin the heart motif in
place and attach using blanket stitch
(see page 152) and a length of
matching yarn. Weave in all ends.

The body of this cozy knits up quickly in mega-chunky yarn,
and it is lined for extra warmth. The flower design may look complicated,
but is worked by simply casting on and casting off stitches.

Gerbera

Materials

Any mega-chunky wool or wool-mix yarn in denim blue (A)
2 x 50g balls or 1 x 100g ball
Oddment of bright pink DK yarn for petals (B)
Oddment of white 4-ply yarn for flower centre (C)
Cream wool DK yarn for lining (D)
1 x 50g ball
Pair of 6mm (UK4:US10) knitting needles
Pair of 4mm (UK8:US6) knitting needles
Pair of 3.25mm (UK10:US3) knitting needles
Spare needle or stitch holder

Dressmaking pins
Tapestry needle
Length of narrow pink ribbon for tie

Tension

Cozy: 11 sts to 4in (10cm) over st st using 6mm needles.
Only the width is crucial. Use larger or smaller needles if
necessary to obtain the correct tension.
Lining: 20 sts to 4in (10cm) over st st using 4mm needles.
Only the width is crucial.

Tip
*Using the cable cast-on method
(see page 138) for this design
creates a good firm edge with a
twisted rope effect.*

Sides
Side 1
*Using 6mm needles and yarn A, cast
on 27 sts and work 3½in (9cm) in st st,
slipping the first st of every row to
produce a tidy edge. Adjust length at
this point if necessary*. Break yarn
and set aside sts on a spare needle
or stitch holder.

Side 2
Work as side 1 from * to *. Do not
break yarn. Knit across sts on needle,
then knit across set-aside sts of side 1
(54 sts).
Next row: Purl.
Next row: (K7, k2tog) across row
(48 sts).
Next row: Purl.
Next row: (K6, k2tog) across row
(42 sts).
Cont as set, decreasing on every alt
row until 18 sts rem.

Next row: Purl.

Next row (eyelets): K2, (yf, k2tog) to end.

Next row: Purl.

Next row: Inc in every st (36 sts). Beg with a knit row, work 6 rows of rev st st on these 36 sts. Cast off loosely.

Flower petals

Using 4mm needles and yarn B, cast on 11 sts, then cast them off immediately, *using loop left on needle, cast on 11 sts and cast them off immediately; rep from * 18 times. Break off yarn leaving a long thread, run through base of each petal in turn and draw up. Fan out petals, pin to front of work and sew in place.

Flower centre

Using 3.25mm needles and yarn C and leaving a long end, cast on 6 sts.

Next row: Inc in each st (12 sts).

Next row: K to end.

Next row: (K1, inc in next st) to end (18 sts).

Next row: Knit.

Break off yarn and thread through all sts. Run long end through sts at cast-on end, join into a circle, pull tight and secure. Now pull the length of yarn threaded through the sts into a circle and secure. Sew in place in centre of the petals.

Lining (make 2)

Using 4mm needles and yarn D, cast on 48 sts using cable cast-on and work 3in (7.5cm) in st st, ending on a purl row.

Next row: (K10, k2tog) across row (44 sts).

Next row: Purl across.

Next row: (K9, k2tog) across row (40 sts).

Next row: Purl across.

Cont as set until 12 sts rem. Cast off.

Making up

Join the lower side edges of the work for approx ¾in (2cm). Join the top side edges for approx 4in (10cm). Join the top and bottom side edges of the lining sections. Turn the work inside out and catch the lining neatly in place just inside the edges of the cozy. Turn the work right side out, thread the ribbon through the eyelets and tie in a bow, allowing the top section to roll over. Weave in all ends.

The harlequin-pattern diamonds on this tea cozy are worked using intarsia (see page 144). Eyelets are worked near the top of the cozy to allow a plaited cord to be threaded through to draw the cozy closed.

Harlequin

Materials

Debbie Bliss Cashmerino Aran, 55% wool, 33% microfibre, 12% cashmere (98yds/90m per 50g)
1 x 50g ball in 101 Ecru (A)
1 x 50g ball in 09 Grey (B)
1 x 50g ball in 50 Lilac (C)
1 x 50g ball in 10 Teal (D)
1 x 50g ball in 34 Gold (E)
Pair of 5mm (UK6:US8) knitting needles
Embroidery needle
Tapestry needle

Tension

18 sts and 24 rows to 4in (10cm) over st st using 5mm needles. Use larger or smaller needles if necessary to obtain the correct tension.

Special abbreviations

MB: Make bobble – k1, yf, k1, yf, k1 into next st, turn, p5, turn, k5, turn, p5, turn, k2tog, k1, k2tog, turn, p3tog, k into back of bobble

Harlequin chart

☐ A 101 Ecru	■ C 50 Lilac
▨ B 09 Grey	■ D 10 Teal

1 square represents 1 stitch and 1 row

Sides (make 2)

Using 5mm needles and E, cast on 44 sts.

Work ½in (1cm) in g st.

Break off F, join in B.

Start chart.

Row 1: K1 B, (work 14 sts row 1 of chart) three times, k1 A.

Row 2: P1 A, (work 14 sts row 2 chart) three times, k1 B.

These 2 rows set the pattern. Cont to follow chart until 36 rows have been completed.

With A, work 5 rows in st st, starting with a knit row.

Next row: Knit.

Eyelet row (RS facing): K3, (k2tog, yf, k4) 6 times, k2tog, yf, k3.

Work 3 rows in g st.

Break off A, join in E.

Work 2 rows in g st.

Cast off as follows:

Cast of 3 sts, MB in next st, (cast off 7 sts including 2 sts on right hand needle, MB in next st) five times, cast off rem sts.

Weave in all ends.

Making up

Sew the side seams, leaving gaps for the handle and spout.

Using E, embroider a French knot (see page 152) in the centre of each diamond.

Cut six strands of yarn 30in (75cm) long and make into a plait. Thread through eyelets.

This cozy is simple to knit but can be decorated with buttons, beads or knitted flowers to give a personal finish. The knitted flowers are held on by coloured brads so they can be removed when you want to wash the cozy.

Country garden

Materials

Any DK yarn

1 x 50g ball in dark green (A)

1 x 50g ball in light green (B)

1 x 50g ball in blue (C)

1 x 50g ball in yellow (D)

Oddments of DK yarn for flowers

Pair of 4mm (UK8:US6) knitting needles

Pair of 3mm (UK11:US–) knitting needles

Buttons and beads as desired

4 x 8mm coloured brads for the flower centres

Tapestry needle

Tension

24 sts and 32 rows to 4in (10cm) over st st using 4mm needles. Use larger or smaller needles if necessary to obtain the correct tension.

Sides

Side 1

Using 4mm needles and A, cast on 38 sts.

Row 1: (K1, p1) to end.

Change to B.

Row 2: (P1, k1) to end.

Row 3: (K1, p1) to end.

Change to A.

Row 4: (P1, k1) to end.

Row 5: (K1, p1) to end.

Rep rows 2–5 until work measures 3in (7.5cm).

Using A, cont in g st for another ¾in (2cm) ending on WS.

Change to C.

Next row (RS): K3, *(k2tog, k5); rep from * to end (33 sts).

Next row: Purl.

Beg with a knit row, work 4 rows in st st**.

Break yarn.

Side 2

Work as side 1 to **. Do not break yarn.

Next row (RS): Knit across all sts from both sides (66 sts).

Next row: *(k2tog, k4); rep from * to end (55 sts).

Next row: Purl.

Next row: *(k2tog, k3); rep from * to end (44 sts).

Next row: Purl.

Next row: *(k2tog, k2); rep from * to end (33 sts).

Next row: Purl.

Next row: *(k2tog, k1); rep from * to end (22 sts).

Next row: Purl.

Change to D.

Next row: K2tog to end (11 sts).

Next row: Purl.

Next row: K1, *(k2tog); rep from * to end (6 sts).

Next row: Purl.

Cut yarn and draw through sts.

Flowers (make 4)

Using 3mm needles and yarn oddment, cast on 16 sts.

Next row: P2tog to end.

Cut yarn, thread through sts, draw together tightly and sew flower ends.

Making up

Join the sides of the cozy together to suit your teapot.

Using yellow yarn, make a pompom (see page 151); sew to the top of cozy. Insert a brad through the centre of each flower and attach them to the cozy.

Sew on buttons and beads. Weave in all ends.

This beautiful cozy with elaborate poppy flowers will bring a sense of luxury to the tea table. The lining gives it extra insulation to keep your tea piping hot.

Black poppy

Materials
Wendy Supreme Luxury Cotton DK, 100% mercerised cotton (219yds/201m per 100g ball)
2 x 100g balls in 1949 Poppy Red (A)
King Cole Bamboo Cotton DK, 50% bamboo viscose, 50% cotton (252yds/230m per 100g ball)
1 x 100g ball in 534 Black (B)
Pair of 4.5mm (UK7:US7) knitting needles
Pair of 3.75mm (UK9:US5) knitting needles
4mm (UK8:USG/6) crochet hook
Spare needle or stitch holder
Small amount of wadding or wool tops for stuffing
Tapestry needle

Tension
19 sts and 23 rows to 4in (10cm) over main pattern using Wendy Supreme Luxury Cotton DK yarn double and 4.5mm needles. Use larger or smaller needles if necessary to obtain the correct tension.

Pattern note

The main body of the tea cozy and the lining are made with the yarn held double.

Body and lining (make 2)

Using 4.5mm needles and yarn A held double, cast on 37 sts.

Row 1: P1, *k1 tbl, p1; rep from * to last st, p1.

Row 2: Knit.

These 2 rows form pattern.

Rep rows 1–2 18 more times ending with row 2 and RS facing for next row.

Transfer these sts to a spare needle or stitch holder.

Work second side of cozy the same, then place both pieces side by side and work joining row.

Joining row: Work 36 sts in pattern across first piece then purl last st and first st on second piece tog, cont in patt to end of row (73 sts).

Shape top

Row 1: P1, *skpo; rep from * to end (37 sts).

Row 2: Knit.

Rep these 2 rows three times more until 6 sts rem. Break yarn leaving a long tail, thread tail through these sts and fasten off securely.

Work the lining of tea cozy in the same way.

Poppy bases (make 7)

Using 4mm hook and B, and leaving a long tail, make 39ch.

Row 1: 1tr into 6th ch from hook, *1ch, miss 2ch, (1tr, 2ch, 1tr) into next ch; rep from * to end.

Row 2: 3ch (counts as 1tr), (1tr, 2ch, 2tr) into first ch sp, *1ch, (2tr, 2ch, 2tr) into next 2ch sp; rep from * to end of row.

Row 3: 3ch (counts as 1tr), 5tr into first 2ch sp, (1dc into next 1ch sp, 6tr into next 2ch sp) twice, (1dc into next 1ch sp, 8tr into next 2ch sp) four times, (1dc into next 1ch sp, 10tr into next 2ch sp) five times.

Fasten off and sew in small end. Starting at centre with long tail, form poppy by coiling straight edge loosely around centre, catching down as you go. Do not cut yarn; leave at back of flower.

Poppy centres (make 7)

Using 3.75mm needles and A, cast on 10 sts.

Row 1: Purl.

Row 2: Inc into every st (20 sts).

Work 7 rows in st st.

Next row: K2tog across row (10 sts). Leave a long tail and break yarn. Using a tapestry needle, run tail through all sts before sliding them off the needle, pull to gather tight and fasten securely. Sew up seam, stuff and then make a gathering stitch around base to close. Sew into centre of poppy base. With long tail of black yarn, come up where centre joins base then go down through hole in middle of centre. Repeat this seven more times equally round centre. Fasten off and weave in ends.

Making up

Join the side seams of the tea cozy and lining, leaving an opening for the handle and the spout.

Attach three poppies to each side of the tea cozy evenly and one in the centre at the top.

Finally, place the lining into the tea cozy with WS facing and slip stitch around the handle and spout openings and around the hem. Weave in all ends.

Tip

It will be easier to arrange and attach the decorations to the tea cozy if you place it over a teapot first.

This design has a separate button-on top, so it is easy to gain access to the lid to refresh your brew without taking the whole cozy off the pot. The buttons are an attractive design detail.

All buttoned up

Materials

Stylecraft Nature's Way Chunky, 100% undyed virgin wool (87yds/80m per 50g ball)

2 × 50g balls in 3652

Pair of 5mm (UK6:US8) knitting needles

Spare needle or stitch holder

4 × 25–30mm buttons

Tapestry needle

Tension

Four repeats of the cable pattern (over 24 sts) measure 5in (12.5cm) wide using 5mm needles. Use larger or smaller needles if necessary to obtain the correct tension.

Special abbreviations

Cab4b: Slip two stitches onto cable needle and hold at back of work, k2, then knit stitches from cable needle

Cab4f: Slip two stitches onto cable needle and hold at front of work, k2, then knit stitches from cable needle

Sides (make 2)

Using 5mm needles, cast on 31 sts and work 4 rows in g st.

Next row: (K3, inc in next st); rep to last 3 sts, k3 (38 sts).

Next row: Knit across.

Next row: K2, (p4, k2); rep to end. Rep last 2 rows once more.

Cable pattern

Row 1: (K2, cab4f, k2, cab4b); rep to last 2 sts, k2.

Row 2: (K2, p4) to last 2 sts, k2.

Row 3: Knit across.

Row 4: As row 2.

Row 5: As row 3.

Row 6: As row 2.

Rep 6 rows of cable pattern until work measures approx 4in (10cm) or the height necessary to suit your pot, ending on row 5 if possible.

Next row: (K2tog, p4); rep to last 2 sts, k2tog (31 sts).

Break off yarn, leaving a long end for making up. Leave sts on a spare needle or stitch holder. Make another piece the same but do not break off yarn; cont on same sts.

Join sides

Keeping to cable pattern (k1, cab4f, k1, cab4b), work across sts on needle to last st. Knit together this last st and the first st of the sts of side 2 to join. Work across sts of side 2, keeping to cable pattern (61 sts).

Next 3 rows: Work in g st.

Cast off, leaving a long end.

Top

Using 5mm needles, cast on 26 sts and work 4 rows in g st.

Next row: K4, cast off 2 sts, k to last 6 sts, cast off 2 sts, k to end.

Next row: K3, p1, cast on 2 sts, p to last 6 sts, cast on 2 sts, p1, k3.

Next row: Knit across.

Next row: K3, p to last 3 sts, k3.

Rep last 2 rows until work measures 3in (7.5cm).

Next row: K11, cast off 4, k to end.

Next row: K3, p to last 3 sts casting on 4 sts over the sts cast off on previous row, k3.

Next row: Knit across.

Next row: K3, p to last 3 sts, k3.

Rep last 2 rows until work measures 2in (5cm) from hole in centre.

Next row: K4, cast off 2 sts, k to last 6 sts, cast off 2 sts, k to end.

Next row: K3, p1, cast on 2 sts, p to last 6 sts, cast on 2 sts, p1, k3.

Work 3 rows in g st. Cast off.

Making up

Join the garter-stitch sections at the top and bottom of the cozy. Work blanket stitch (see page 152) loosely round hole in lid.

Place the cozy and the lid on the pot and work out the position for the buttons.

Sew on buttons. Weave in all ends.

> ## Tip
> *The height of this cover is important for a snug fit, so measure your pot before shaping the top.*

This tea cozy crocheted in shell stitch has an elegant vintage vibe.
Choose your stripe colours to complement a favourite tea set
and finish off the project with a co-ordinating button.

Shell-pattern stripes

Materials

Rico Design Essentials Merino DK, 100% merino wool
(131yds/120m per 50g ball)
1 × 50g ball in 005 Red (A)
1 × 50g ball in 098 Silver Grey (B)
4mm (UK8:USG/6) crochet hook
2 × 4mm (UK8:US6) double-pointed needles to make I-cord
1 × 1¼in (3.5cm) button
Tapestry needle

Tension

5 V shell sts and 10 rows to 4in (10cm) over V shell pattern
using 4mm hook. Use a larger or smaller hook if necessary to
obtain the correct tension.

Sides (make 2)

Row 1: Using 4mm hook and A, make 36ch.

Row 2: (2tr, 1ch, 2tr) into 6th ch from hook, *miss 2ch, (2tr, 1ch, 2tr) in next ch; rep from * to last 3 sts, miss 2ch, 1tr in last ch, turn (10 V shell clusters).

Row 3: 3ch, *(2tr, 1ch, 2tr) into 1 ch sp; rep from * to end, 1tr in 3rd ch of turning ch, turn (10 V shell clusters).

Row 3 forms the pattern. Follow the following colour sequence:

Row 4: Change to B, rep row 3.

Rows 5–6: Change to A, rep row 3.

Row 7: Change to B, rep row 3.

Rows 8–9: Change to A, rep row 3.

Row 10: Change to B, rep row 3.

Row 11: Change to A, 3ch, 1tr into first shell ch sp, *(2tr, 1ch, 2tr) into next 1 ch sp; rep from * seven times, 1tr in last shell ch sp, 1tr in 3rd ch of turning ch, turn (8 V shell clusters).

Row 12: 3ch, *(2tr, 1ch, 2tr) into 1 ch sp; rep from * to end, 1tr in 3rd ch of turning ch, turn (8 V shell clusters).

Row 13: Change to B, 3ch, 1tr into first shell ch sp, *(2tr, 1ch, 2tr) into next 1 ch sp; rep from * five times, 1tr in last shell ch sp, 1tr in 3rd ch of turning ch, turn (6 V shell clusters).

Row 14: Change to A, 3ch, *(2tr, 1ch, 2tr) into 1 ch sp; rep from * to end, 1tr in 3rd ch of turning ch, turn (6 V shell clusters).

Row 15: 3ch, 1tr into first shell ch sp, *(2tr, 1ch, 2tr) into next 1 ch sp; rep from * three times, 1tr in last shell ch sp, 1tr in 3rd ch of turning ch, turn (4 V shell clusters).

Row 16: Change to B, ch 3, *(2 tr, 1ch, 2 tr) into 1 ch sp; rep from * to end, 1 tr in 3rd ch of turning ch, turn (4 V shell clusters).

Row 17: Change to A, 1tr into first shell ch sp, *(2tr, 1ch, 2tr) into next 1 ch sp; rep from * once, 1tr in last shell ch sp, 1tr in 3rd ch of turning ch, turn (2 V shell clusters). Fasten off and weave in ends.

Making up

Using A and 4mm hook, attach yarn at the bottom right-hand edge and dc along the sides and over the top of each tea cozy side.

Join seams using either slip stitch or backstitch, leaving spaces for spout and handle opening.

Using A and 4mm hook, attach yarn at the base of the tea cozy and dc in each ch st around the bottom edge of the tea cozy. Fasten off and weave in ends. Make a 12in (30cm) I-cord using B and two 4mm double-pointed knitting needles. Make three loops and secure firmly to the top of the tea cozy using a tapestry needle. Then secure a button in the centre.

This charming owl made in a crocheted cluster pattern will bring a smile to everyone's face at the breakfast table. Sewn-on buttons enhance the roundness of his eyes, and the chirpy beak adds character.

Owl

Materials

Rico Design Fashion Nature DK, 80% acrylic, 10% wool, 5% alpaca, 5% viscose (254yds/233m per 50g ball)

1 x 50g ball in 008 Camel (A)

1 x 50g ball in 001 Beige (B)

Rico Design Essentials Merino DK, 100% merino wool (131yds/120m per 50g ball)

Small amount in 023 Grey Blue (C)

Rico Design Essentials Soft Merino Aran, 100% merino wool (109yds/100m per 50g ball)

Small amount in 070 Mandarin (D)74mm (UK8:USG/6) crochet hook

3.5mm (UK9:USE/4) crochet hook

2 x ½in (1.25cm) buttons

Tapestry needle

Sewing needle

Sewing thread in co ordinating colour

Tension

9 V granite clusters sts and 18 rows to 4in (10cm) over V granite pattern using 4mm hook and Rico Design Fashion Nature DK. Use a larger or smaller hook if necessary to obtain the correct tension.

Special abbreviations

MC: Magic circle (see page 148)

Tea cozy sides (make 2)

Row 1: Using 4mm hook and A, make 36ch.

Row 2: (1dc, 1ch, 1dc) in 3rd ch from hook, *miss 1ch, (1dc, 1ch, 1dc) in next ch; rep from * to last ch st, 1dc in last ch, turn (17 V shell clusters).

Row 3: 1ch, *1dc, 1ch, 1dc into 1 ch sp of next cluster; rep from * to end, 1dc in turning ch, turn (17 V clusters). Row 3 forms the pattern. Follow the following colour sequence:

Rows 4–6: Work 3 rows in patt.

Rows 7–9: Change to B, work 3 rows in patt.

Rows 10–14: Change to A, work 5 rows in patt.

Rows 15–17: Change to B, work 3 rows in patt.

Rows 18–22: Change to A, work 5 rows in patt.

Row 23: Change to B, 1ch, 1dc into first ch sp, *(1dc, 1ch, 1dc) into 1 ch sp of next cluster; rep from * 14 times, 1dc in last ch sp, 1dc in turning ch, turn (15 V clusters).

Row 24: 1ch, miss 1dc *(1dc, 1ch, 1dc) into 1 ch sp of next cluster; rep from * in rest of ch sps, miss 1dc, 1dc in turning ch, turn (15 V clusters).

Row 25: 1ch, *(1dc, 1ch, 1dc) into 1 ch sp of next cluster; rep from * to

end, 1dc in turning ch, turn (15 V clusters).

Row 26: Change to A, 1ch, 1dc into first ch sp, *(1dc, 1ch, 1dc) into 1 ch sp of next cluster; rep from * to last ch sp, 1dc in last ch sp, 1dc in turning ch, turn (13 V clusters).

Row 27: 1ch, miss 1dc *(1dc, 1ch, 1dc) into 1 ch sp of next cluster; rep from * in rest of ch sps, miss 1dc, 1dc in turning ch, turn (13 V clusters).

Row 28: 1ch, 1dc into first ch sp, *(1dc, 1ch, 1dc) into 1 ch sp of next cluster; rep from * to last ch sp, 1dc in last ch sp, 1dc in turning ch, turn (11 V clusters).

Row 29: 1ch, miss 1dc *(1dc, 1ch, 1dc) into 1 ch sp of next cluster; rep from * in rest of ch sps, miss 1dc, 1dc in turning ch, turn (11 V clusters).

Row 30: 1ch, 1dc into first ch sp, *(1dc, 1ch, 1dc) into 1 ch sp of next cluster; rep from * to last ch sp, 1dc in last ch sp, 1dc in turning ch, turn (9 V clusters).

Row 31: 1ch, miss 1dc *(1dc, 1ch, 1dc) into 1 ch sp of next cluster; rep from * in rest of ch sps, miss 1dc, 1dc in turning ch, turn (9 V clusters). Fasten off and weave in ends.

Eyes (make 2)

Round 1: With 3.5mm hook and C make an MC, work 8dc, sl st in first dc to join (8 sts).

Round 2: 3ch, 1tr in same st, 2tr into each st, join with sl st (16 sts).

Round 3: Change to B, 3ch, 1tr in same st, 1tr in next st, * 2tr in next st, 1tr in next st; rep from * six times, sl st in 3rd ch, join with sl st (24 sts). Fasten off and weave in ends.

Beak

Row 1: With 4mm hook and D, make 2ch.

Row 2: 2dc in 2nd ch from hook, turn (2 sts).

Row 3: 1ch, 2dc in each st, turn (4 sts).

Row 4: 1ch, 2dc in first st, 1dc in next 2 sts, 2dc in last st, turn (6 sts).

Row 5: 1ch, dc to end, turn (6 sts).

Row 6: 1ch, dc to end (6 sts). Fasten off and weave in ends.

Making up

Join seams using either slip stitch or whip stitch (see page 150), leaving spaces for the spout and handle openings.

Place eyes on one side of the tea cozy and, using co-ordinating thread, sew to the tea cozy using whip stitch.

Using co-ordinating thread, sew a button to the centre of each eye.

Using co-ordinating yarn, sew the beak to the same side of the tea cozy using whip stitch.

The hearts on this cozy are created using the intarsia colourwork technique (see page 144). The yarn is an aran-weight to give the cozy some substance and keep your tea deliciously hot.

Love hearts

Materials

Rowan Pure Wool Aran, 100% wool
(186yds/170m per 100g ball)
1 × 100g ball in 670 Ivory (A)
1 × 100g ball in 679 Ember (B)
Pair of 5mm (UK6:US8) knitting needles
Pair of 4mm (UK8:US6) knitting needles
Tapestry needle

Tension

18 sts and 24 rows to 4in (10cm) over st st using 5mm needles. Use larger or smaller needles if necessary to obtain the correct tension.

Sides (make 2)

Using 5mm needles and B, cast on 43 sts.

Knit 3 rows.

Join in A and work 2 rows in st st.

Starting with row 1 of chart, follow until completed, shaping as shown on chart.

Cast off.

Hearts (make 5)

Using B and 4mm needles, cast on 2 sts.

Row 1: Inc in both sts (4 sts).

Row 2 (and every following alternate row): Knit.

Row 3: K1, M1, k2, M1, k1 (6 sts).

Row 5: K1, M1, k4, M1, k1 (8 sts).

Knit 3 rows.

Row 9: K2tog, k4, k2tog (6 sts).

Row 10: K1, k2tog, turn, cast off.

Join yarn to rem sts, k2tog, k1.

Cast off, leaving a length of yarn to sew to cozy.

Making up

Sew up side seams, leaving openings for the handle and the spout. Sew up the top seam.

Sew three of the hearts on top of the cozy, pulling through the yarn to secure.

Tie

Using three strands of B, 20in (50cm) long, make a plait. Secure to the top under the hearts, and then sew the remaining two hearts onto the ends of the plait. Weave in all ends.

Love Hearts chart

□ A 670 Ivory

■ B 679 Ember

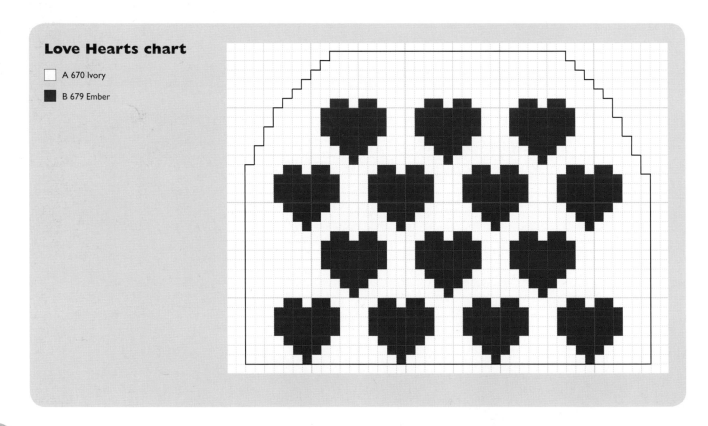

Light-dappled water, waterlilies, and the fleeting iridescence of a dragonfly.
This tea cozy, inspired by Monet's famous paintings of waterlilies,
will bring a touch of summer to any tea-time table, even in winter.

Monet

Materials

Hayfield Bonus DK, 100% acrylic (306yds/280m per 100g ball)

1 x 100g ball in 0904 Orchard (A)

1 x 100g ball in 0958 Light Pink (B)

Patons Dreamtime 2 Ply, 100% wool (372yds/340m per 50g ball)

Small quantity of 0051 White (C) (alternatively, organdie or
satin ribbon or felt, cut to shape to mimic dragonfly wings,
could be used)

Pair of 3.75mm (UK9:US5) knitting needles

Set of 5 x 3.75mm (UK9:US5) double-pointed needles

2 x 3.25mm (UK10:US3) and 2 x 2.5mm (UK12:US–)
double-pointed needles to make I-cord

Fine crochet hook (optional)

4 x ⅛in (4mm) teal beads

6 x ⅛in (4mm) gold beads

Beading needle

Clear sewing thread

Dressmaking pins

Tapestry needle

Tension

22 sts and 25 rows to 4in (10cm) over st st using
3.75mm needles and Hayfield Bonus DK yarn. Use larger
or smaller needles if necessary to obtain the correct tension.

Special abbreviations

Kfb: Knit into the front and back of the next stitch

PB: Place bead by slipping a stitch as it comes off the left needle (purlwise) and onto the right, pushing a bead up the yarn as close to the slipped stitch as possible without slack, then knit the next stitch to secure the bead

Pattern notes

The basic cozy is knitted in four simple stages, then each waterlily is worked, followed by the I-cord with the dragonflies. Leave long cast-on and cast-off tails throughout, as they will be used for sewing up. Unless otherwise directed, use the thumb cast-on method throughout (see page 139).

Basic leaf border

With 3.75mm needles and A, and using thumb method, cast on 8 sts.

Row 1 (RS): K5, yf, k1, yf, k2 (10 sts).
Row 2: P6, kfb, k3 (11 sts).
Row 3: K4, p1, k2, yf, k1, yf, k3 (13 sts).
Row 4: P8, kfb, k4 (14 sts).
Row 5: K4, p2, k3, yf, k1, yf, k4 (16 sts).
Row 6: P10, kfb, k5 (17 sts).
Row 7: K4, p3, k4, yf, k1, yf, k5 (19 sts).
Row 8: P12, kfb, k6 (20 sts).
Row 9: K4, p4, sl1, k1, psso, k7, k2tog, k1 (18 sts).
Row 10: P10, kfb, k7 (19 sts).

Row 11: K4, p5, sl1, k1, psso, k5, k2tog, k1 (17 sts).
Row 12: P8, kfb, k2, p1, k5 (18 sts).
Row 13: K4, p1, k1, p4, sl1, k1, psso, k3, k2tog, k1 (16 sts).
Row 14: P6, kfb, k3, p1, k5 (17 sts).
Row 15: K4, p1, k1, p5, sl1, k1, psso, k1, k2tog, k1 (15 sts).
Row 16: P4, kfb, k4, p1, k5 (16 sts).
Row 17: K4, p1, k1, p6, sl1, k2tog, psso, k1 (14 sts).
Row 18 (WS): P2tog, cast off next 5 sts using p2tog st to cast off first st, p3, k4 (8 sts).

Rep rows 1–18 six times more (7 leaves in total). Cast off.

Sides (make 2)

Pin the leaf border in a circle, RS together and sew up along the garter-st border for around ¾in (2cm) to form a ring. Turn RS out and fold in half with seam just made to the right. Using 3.75mm needles and A, pick up 48 sts evenly on the first half. (It is sometimes easier to do this with a crochet hook, putting them onto the needle one by one facing correctly for a knit row. This is optional; otherwise pick up using the preferred method.)

Row 1 (WS): K4, p to last 4 sts, k4.
Row 2: K4, *p1, k3; rep from * to last 4 sts, k4.
Row 3: K4, *k1, p5, k1, p1; rep from * to last 4 sts, k4.
Row 4: K4, *k2, p1, k3, p1, k1; rep from * to last 4 sts, k4.
Row 5: K4, *p2, k1, p1, k1, p3; rep from * to last 4 sts, k4.

Rep rows 2–5 six times more (7 repeats in all).

With RS facing, put sts onto 3.75mm dpns.

Join sides

Round 1: *P1, k3; rep from * to end of round (96 sts).
Round 2: K3, p1, * k1, p1, k5, p1; rep from * to last 4 sts, k1, p1, k2.
Round 3: K2, p1, k1, *k2, p1, k3, p1, k1; rep from * to last 4 sts, k2, p1, k1.
Round 4: K1, p1, k2, *k3, p1, k1, p1, k2; rep from * to last 4 sts, k3, p1.

Rep rounds 1–4 three more times.

Eyelets

Round 1: Purl.
Round 2: Knit.
Round 3: *K2, yf, k2tog; rep from * to end of round.

Round 4: Knit.
Round 5: Purl.

Picot edging
Rounds 1–2: Knit.
Round 3: *Yf, k2tog; rep from *
to end.
Rounds 4–6: Knit.
Cast off k-wise, leaving a long tail, and
break yarn.
Fold the picot in half to the inside of
the cozy, being careful to ensure that
the picots match to provide an even
crenulation. Pin into place, then catch
the sts down, so that no sts show
on RS.

Waterlilies (make 6)
These are made in one long piece of
five small petals then five larger ones.
The large ones form the centre, while
the small petals make the splayed
outer section.
With 3.25mm dpns and B, cast on
7 sts.

Small petals
Row 1: Purl.
Row 2: Knit.
Row 3: Purl.
Row 4: Cast off 5 sts knit-wise, leaving
2 sts on the needles, knit the last st.
Row 5: Purl.
Row 6: Put the right needle
through the first stitch and knit a stitch

(3 stitches on the needle). Cast on 4 sts using cable cast-on method (see page 138) and knit the row (7 sts). Rep rows 1–6 four more times so that there are five small petals in all ending on a row 5.

Large petals

Row 1: Put right needle into first stitch, knit a stitch (3 stitches on the needle). Cast on 5 sts using cable cast-on method and knit the row (8 sts).
Row 2: Purl.
Row 3: Knit.
Row 4: Purl.
Row 5: Cast off 6 sts with 2 rem on the needle, k the last st, turn.
Row 6: P to the end, turn.

Rep last 6 rows four more times so that there are five large petals in all. On the last large petal when reaching row 5, cast off all 8 sts and fasten off, leaving a long tail.

I-Cord and Dragonflies

The I-cord and dragonfly bodies are made in one piece with the wings knitted separately and pushed through the body afterwards. The right and left wings are made in one piece, large and small. Make two large and two small, pairing them as directed.

Small wings (make 2)

Using 2.5mm dpns and C, cast on 17 sts.

Row 1 (WS): P to end.
Row 2: (SI1, k1, psso) twice, k to the last 4 sts, (k2tog) twice (13 sts).
Row 3: P to end.
Row 4: (SI1, k1, psso) three times to last 6 sts, (k2tog) three times (7 sts).
Row 5: Cast off p-wise.

Large wings (make 2)

Using 2.5mm dpns and C, cast on 21 sts.
Row 1 (WS): P to end.
Row 2: (SI1, k1, psso) twice, k to the last 4 sts, (k2tog) twice (17 sts).
Row 3: P to end.
Row 4: (SI1, k1, psso) four times, k to last 8 sts, (k2tog) four times (9 sts).
Row 5: Cast off p-wise.

I-Cord

Thread four teal beads onto yarn A. With 2.5mm dpns, cast on 4 sts and make I-cord that measures 1¼in (3.5cm).

Change to 3.25mm dpns and work as before until the I-cord measures 2½in (6cm).

Next row (first dragonfly): K1, M1R, k3 (5 sts).
Row 2: K1, PB, k1, PB, k1.
Row 3: K1 to end (as I-cord).
Row 4: SI1, k1, psso, k1, k2tog (3 sts). Change to 2.5mm dpns and knit backwards and forwards without turning until work measures

24½in (62cm) excluding the dragonfly just worked.

Change to 3.25mm dpns.

Next row (second dragonfly): K1, MIR, k1, MIL, k1 (5 sts).

Next row: K to end.

Next row: K1, PB, k1, PB, k1.

K (as I-cord) for a further 1in (2.5cm). Change to 2.5mm dpns.

Next row: Sl1, k1, psso, k3 (4 sts).

K (as I-cord) and work for a further 1¼in (3.5cm).

Cast off, leaving a long tail.

Making up
Wings

Start at top right-hand corner of the large wings. With a yarn tail weave the yarn around the wing edges, gathering only slightly. Fasten off. Repeat with the other large wing and then the small wings. Take the large wings again and with the yarn tail at the bottom left, run it along the back of the wing to the centre. Both wings should have their curves pointing downwards. Place the smaller wing centrally on top, balancing its top edge on the lower edge on the large wing. Pin into place and attach the smaller wing to the large one neatly. To do this, use the bottom left yarn tail on the smaller wing running it along its edge approximately halfway, and ruche both wings slightly. Fasten off. Repeat with the other wings.

I-cord

Draw the yarn tail up through the centre of the I-cord for approx 1½in (3.5cm) of tail, work some running stitches around the body in a circle at this point and pull tight. At 1½in (3.5cm) from the bottom of the tail, place the wings by drawing them gently through the body horizontally, using a crochet hook or preferred method. Pull the yarn tail up through the body again for approx 1in (2.5cm) and repeat the running stitches as above. Repeat this once more, taking the yarn tail to one row above the eyes and work some running stitches in a circle and pull tight. Run the yarn inside the I-cord for a few rows, catch it down, run it back again and fasten off so that the cut yarn does not show. Repeat this at the other end, using the first dragonfly as a template for the second one, to ensure that the tail, body and head divides are evenly executed.

Waterlilies

Thread the long yarn tail onto a tapestry needle and work the yarn around each petal to the base of every one from the first large petal to the last small one, gently gathering them to form delicate curves. Fasten off. With the other yarn tail, thread along the base of the petals gathering this to form a flower. The petals may twist in on themselves at this point; if this happens, just untwist them. The five large ones should form the centre with one in the middle and four around it. The five small ones will form a flower shape, cradling the larger centre. Draw the yarn tails neatly through the central hole formed by the gathers, fasten off, then trim. Repeat until all the flowers are complete.

Cozy

Weave in any loose ends and fasten off neatly. With leaf border seam to the right, thread the I-cord through the eyelets so that the tail ends are centrally placed at the front for tying, allowing the dragonflies to 'hover' above the pond. Gather and tie. Place over a teapot, balled towel or similar. Thread a beading needle with invisible thread and pick up a gold bead. Pin the first lily in place and attach with the bead in the centre, running a few stitches underneath the lily pad, fasten off and cut. Repeat with the other lilies, placing them evenly. Remember not to start with the lily pad under the spout, as this is impractical! Start centrally and flank one lily on either side of it.

This pattern, with its profusion of tea roses, creates a very special and luxurious cozy that is sure to become a treasured item. The lining ensures that you'll have a well-insulated teapot.

Tea roses

Materials
Wendy Supreme Luxury Cotton DK, 100% mercerized cotton (219yds/201m per 100g ball)
2 x 100g balls in 1851 Cream (A)
Woolyknit DK Classics, 100% merino wool (106yds/96m per 50g ball)
12 x 50g balls in Red (B)
1 x 50g ball in Forest (C)
Pair of 4.5mm (UK7:US7) knitting needles
Spare needle or stitch holder
Tapestry needle

Tension
19 sts and 23 rows to 4in (10cm) over main pattern using Wendy Supreme Luxury Cotton DK yarn double and 4.5mm needles. Use larger or smaller needles if necessary to obtain the correct tension.

Pattern notes

Note that the body and lining of
the cozy are made with yarn A held
double. The flowers and leaves are
knitted and then placed in a net
bag, washing bag or pillowcase and
lightly felted in a washing machine at
100–120°F (40–50°C), depending on
your machine. It is advisable to test a
sample first to achieve the best results.
If the pieces don't come out felted
enough the first time, put them back in,
maybe at a higher temperature.
However, do not over-felt as the petals
will fuse together.

Body and lining
(make 2)

Using 4.5mm needles and double
strand of A, cast on 37 sts.
Row 1: P1, *k1 tbl, p1; rep from * to
last st, p1.
Row 2: Knit.
These 2 rows form the pattern.

Rep rows 1 and 2, 18 more times,
ending with row 2 and RS facing for
next row. Transfer these sts to a spare
needle or stitch holder.
Work second side of cozy the same,
then place both side by side and work
joining row.
Joining row: Work 36 sts in pattern
across first piece then purl last st and
first st on second piece together, cont
in patt to end of row (73 sts).

Shape top

Row 1: P1, *skpo; rep from * to end
(37 sts).
Row 2: Knit.
Rep these 2 rows three times more
until 6 sts rem. Break yarn, leaving a
long tail; thread tail through these sts
and fasten off securely.
Work the lining of tea cozy in the
same way.

Tea roses (make 37)

Using 4.5mm needles and B, leave a
long tail and cast on 6 sts.

Small petals

Row 1: Purl.
Row 2: Inc, k5 (7 sts).
Row 3: K1, p4, inc, p1 (8 sts).
Row 4: Inc, k7 (9 sts).
Work 4 rows in st st.
Row 9: K1, p5, p2tog, p1 (8 sts).
Row 10: K1, skpo, k5 (7 sts).

Row 11: K1, p3, p2tog, p1 (6 sts).
Rep rows 1–11 another three times
(4 petals). Do not break yarn.

Medium petals

Carrying on from small petals:
Row 1: Inc, k5 (7 sts).
Row 2: K1, p4, inc, p1 (8 sts).
Row 3: Inc, k7 (9 sts).
Row 4: K1, p6, inc, p1 (10 sts).
Row 5: Inc, k9 (11 sts).
Work 4 rows in st st.
Row 10: K1, p7, p2tog, p1 (10 sts).
Row 11: K1, skpo, k7 (9 sts).
Row 12: K1, p5, p2tog, p1 (8 sts).
Row 13: K1, skpo, k5 (7 sts).
Row 14: K1, p3, p2tog, p1 (6 sts).
Rep rows 1–14 twice more (3 petals).
Do not break off yarn.

Large petals

Carrying on from medium petals:

Row 1: Inc, k5 (7 sts).
Row 2: K1, p4, inc, p1 (8 sts).
Row 3: Inc, k7 (9 sts).
Row 4: K1, p6, inc, p1 (10 sts).
Row 5: Inc, k9 (11 sts).
Row 6: K1, p8, inc, p1 (12 sts).
Row 7: Inc, k11 (13 sts).
Work 8 rows in st st.
Row 16: K1, p9, p2tog, p1 (12 sts).
Row 17: K1, skpo, k9 (11 sts).
Row 18: K1, p7, p2tog, p1 (10 sts).
Row 19: K1, skpo, k7 (9 sts).
Row 20: K1, p5, p2tog, p1 (8 sts).
Row 21: K1, skpo, k5 (7 sts).
Row 22: K1, p3, p2tog, p1 (6 sts).
Rep rows 1–22 once more (2 petals).
Next row: Work 4 more rows, dec 1 st every row as above until 2 sts rem. Fasten off.

Using the long end of yarn, starting at centre with the small petals and with the purl side facing outwards, form rose by coiling straight edge around itself. This should form a flat base that you catch together with a tapestry needle as you go. Pull out the centre petals slightly; the outer petals will curve outwards naturally.

Sew in ends, then place in a net bag and felt in a washing machine at 100–120°F (40–50°C).

Leaves (make 6)

Using 4.5mm needles and C, cast on 3 sts.

Row 1 (RS): Knit.
Row 2: Inc twice, k1 (5 sts).
Row 3: K2, yf, sl1 p-wise, yb, k2.
Row 4: K1, inc twice, k2 (7 sts).
Row 5 and every odd row: K to centre st, yf, sl1 p-wise, yb, k to end.
Row 6: K2, inc twice, k3 (9 sts).
Row 8: K3, inc twice, k4 (11 sts).
Row 10: K4, inc twice, k5 (13 sts).
Row 12: K5, inc twice, K6 (15 sts).
Row 14: K6, inc twice, k7 (17 sts).
Work 7 rows in st st.
Row 22: K1, skpo, k11, k2tog, k1 (15 sts).
Row 24: K1, skpo, k9, k2tog, k1 (13 sts).
Row 26: K1, skpo, k7, k2tog, k1 (11 sts).
Row 28: K1, skpo, k5, k2tog, k1 (9 sts).
Row 30: K1, skpo, k3, k2tog, k1 (7 sts).
Row 32: K1, skpo, k1, k2tog, k1 (5 sts).
Row 34: K1, sl2, k1, p2sso, K1 (3 sts).
Row 36: K3tog, fasten off.

Sew in ends, place in a net bag and felt in washing machine at 100–120°F (40–50°C).

Making up

Join side seams of tea cozy and lining, leaving an opening for the handle and for the spout.

Attach the leaves around the top of the tea cozy with cast-on edges together in centre.

Starting at the base of the hem, arrange and attach roses to each side of the cozy as shown here:

```
  •     •     •     •
•    •     •     •    •
  •    •    •    •
```

Place the final rose in the centre of the leaves at the top and sew in place. Finally, place the lining into the tea cozy with wrong sides facing and slip stitch (see page 150) around the handle and spout openings and around the hem. Weave in all ends.

This project is a good introduction to the technique of entrelac, which is easier than it looks. It produces a stunning effect and a substantial cozy to keep your tea piping hot.

Elegant entrelac

Materials

Twilley's Freedom Spirit DK, 100% wool yarn (130yds/119m per 50g ball), or other variegated pure wool DK yarn
1 x 50g ball in 518 Desire (purple mix) (A)
1 x 50g ball in 513 Verve (green mix) (B)
Pair of 4mm (UK8:US6) knitting needles
Tapestry needle

Tension

10 sts and 12 rows to 4in (10cm) over st st using 4mm needles. One repeat of the pattern over 32 sts measures approx 8in (20cm) unstretched. Use larger or smaller needles if necessary to obtain the correct tension.

Entrelac panels (make 2)

Using 4mm needles and A, cast on 40 sts loosely.

Work 8 rows in g st.

Next row (dec): K2, (k2tog, k3); rep to last 3 sts, k2tog, k1 (32 sts).

Change to B.

Base triangles

Row 1: *P2, turn.

Row 2: Sl1, k1, turn.

Row 3: Sl1, p2, turn.

Row 4: Sl1, k2, turn.

Row 5: Sl1, p3, turn.

Row 6: Sl1, k3, turn.

Cont in this way, working 1 more st on each purl row until the row 'Sl1, k6, turn' has been worked.

Next row: Sl1, p7 but do not turn*. Using the next 2 sts on the left-hand needle, rep from * to * to form the second base triangle. Rep twice more, ending sl1, k7, turn (four base triangles worked).

First tier

Change to A to work first tier of three rectangles and two edge triangles.

Right edge triangle

Row 1: K2, turn.

Row 2: Sl1, p1, turn.

Row 3: Inc in first st, skpo, turn.

Row 4: Sl1, p2, turn.

Row 5: Inc in first st, k1, skpo, turn.

Row 6: Sl1, p3, turn.

Row 7: Inc in first st, k2, skpo, turn.

Row 8: Sl1, p4, turn.

Row 9: Inc in first st, k3, skpo, turn.

Cont thus until the row 'inc in first st, k5, skpo' has been worked but do not turn (8 sts).

Next row: **Pick up and knit 8 sts along left edge of next triangle, turn.

Next row: Sl1, p7, turn.

Next row: Sl1, k6, skpo, turn.

Rep last 2 rows until all sts of second triangle have been worked, do not turn** (first rectangle).

Rep from ** to ** twice more, to form two further rectangles.

Left edge triangle

Pick up 8 sts from edge of last triangle.

Row 1: P2tog, p6, turn.

Row 2: Sl1, k6, turn.

Row 3: P2tog, p5, turn.

Row 4: Sl1, k5, turn.

Row 5: P2tog, p4, turn.

Row 6: Sl1, k4, turn.

Row 7: P2tog, p3, turn.

Row 8: Sl1, k3, turn.

Row 9: P2tog, p2, turn.

Row 10: Sl1, k2, turn.
Row 11: P2tog, p1, turn.
Row 12: Sl1, k1, turn.
Row 13: P2tog but do not turn.

Second tier

Join in B. Pick up p-wise and purl 7 sts from side of first triangle, turn (8 sts, including st left on needle from previous row).
Row 1: Sl1, k7, turn.
Row 2: Sl1, p6, p2tog, turn.
Rep last 2 rows until all sts of rectangle have been worked (8 sts) but do not turn. ***Pick up p-wise and purl 8 sts from side of next rectangle, turn. Rep rows 1 and 2 to complete next rectangle***. Rep from *** to *** to complete the final two rectangles of the tier.

Third tier

Join in A.
Row 1: K2, turn.
Row 2: Sl1, p1, turn.
Row 3: Inc in first st, skpo, turn.
Row 4: Sl1, p2, turn.
Row 5: Inc in first st, k1, skpo, turn.
Row 6: Sl1, p3, turn.
Row 7: Inc in first st, k2, skpo, turn.
Row 8: Sl1, p4, turn.
Row 9: Inc in first st, k3, skpo, turn.
Row 10: Sl1, p5, turn.
Row 11: Inc in first st, k4, skpo, turn.
Row 12: Sl1, p6, turn.

Row 13: Inc in first st, k5, skpo (8 sts). Do not turn. Pick up and knit 8 sts from edge of next rectangle, turn.
Next row: Sl1, p7, turn.
Next row: Sl1, k6, skpo, turn.
Rep last 2 rows until all sts of rectangle have been worked. Do not turn. Pick up and knit 8 sts from side of next rectangle and complete in the same way. Rep for final rectangle.

Left edge triangle

Pick up 8 sts from side of last rectangle of previous row and complete as for left edge triangle of first tier.

Final tier

Join in B. Pick up p-wise and purl 7 sts from edge of triangle just worked (8 sts, including st left on needle from previous row).
Row 1: Sl1, k7, turn.
Row 2: P2tog, p5, p2tog, turn.
Row 3: Sl1, k6, turn.
Row 4: P2tog, p4, p2tog, turn.
Row 5: Sl1, k5, turn.
Row 6: P2tog, p3, p2tog, turn.
Row 7: Sl1, k4, turn.
Row 8: P2tog, p2, p2tog, turn.
Row 9: Sl1, k3, turn.
Row 10: P2tog, p1, p2tog, turn.
Row 11: Sl1, k2, turn.
Row 12: P2tog, p2tog, turn.
Row 13: Sl1, k1, turn.
Row 14: P2tog, p2tog, turn.

Row 15: Sl1, k1, turn.
Row 16: P2tog (1 st on needle). Pick up p-wise and purl 7 sts from edge of rectangle of previous tier (8 sts, including st left on needle). Rep last 16 rows three times. Fasten off.

Join panels

Using 4mm needles and A, with RS facing, pick up and knit 40 sts along top edge of first panel, then pick up and knit 40 sts along top edge of second panel.
Purl 1 row.
Next row: (K8, k2tog) across row (72 sts).
Next row: Purl.
Next row: (K7, k2tog) across row (64 sts).
Cont in this way until there are 32 sts on needle, ending with a purl row.
Next row: (K2tog) across row (16 sts).
Join in B and purl across row.
Next row: Inc in every st (32 sts). Work 16 rows in g st. Cast off.

Making up

Join top and bottom side edges of work and weave in ends.
Place on pot, allowing top of work to roll over.

The design of this tea cozy is easy to tackle even if you are a beginner to crochet. You simply make the basic cozy and embroider the heart pattern onto it in cross stitch afterwards.

Cross stitch

Materials

Rico Design Essentials Cotton DK, 100% cotton
(142yds/130m per 50g ball)
1 x 50g ball in 051 Nature (A)
Small amount of red embroidery thread or 4-ply cotton yarn
3.5mm (UK9:USE/4) crochet hook
Stitch markers
2 x ½in (1.25cm) buttons
Tapestry needle

Tension

20 sts and 26 rows to 4in (10cm) over dc using 3.5mm hook. Use a larger or smaller hook if necessary to obtain the correct tension.

Tea cozy

Row 1: Using 3.5mm hook and A, make 50ch.

Row 2 (WS): 1dc in 2nd ch from hook, 1 dc into each ch to end, turn (49 sts).

Row 2 forms the pattern. Work a further 99 rows. Fasten off and weave in ends.

Buttonholes

Fold the crochet work in half and, with a stitch marker, mark each end of the row.

With WS facing, join yarn to the end stitch, 10ch, sl st back into row end. Rep on the other side to create buttonhole loops. Fasten off and weave in ends.

Cross stitch pattern

The crocheted fabric forms the grid on which you will cross stitch. The corners of each 'square' are located on either side of a double crochet, horizontally, and over two rows of double crochet, vertically. Using the chart as a guide, work in cross stitch using red embroidery thread or 4-ply cotton yarn on both sides of the cozy.

Making up

With right sides together, push button loops through to between the right sides of the crochet. Slip stitch both sides of the cozy together. Fasten off and weave in ends. Sew a button either side of the cozy eight rows below the buttonhole loops. Put the button through the buttonholes.

Cross stitch chart

☐ A 051 Nature

■ Red embroidery thread

1 square represents 1 stitch and 2 rows

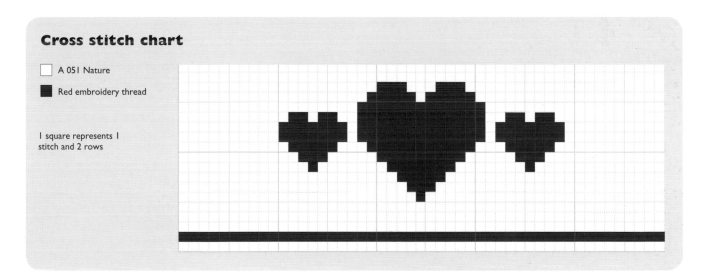

This bright and cheerful tea cozy takes inspiration for its design from traditional Nordic sweater patterns. The colourwork is created using the Fairisle technique (see page 144).

Nordic

Materials

Debbie Bliss Donegal Luxury Tweed Aran, 85% wool, 15% angora (96yds/88m per 50g ball)

1 x 50g ball in 04 Red (A)

1 x 50g ball in 07 Oatmeal (B)

Pair of 5mm (UK6:US8) knitting needles

Tapestry needle

Tension

18 sts and 24 rows to 4in (10cm) over st st using 5mm needles. Use larger or smaller needles if necessary to obtain the correct tension.

Sides (make 2)

Using 5mm needles and B, cast on 46 sts.

Row 1: K2, *p2, k2; rep from * to end.

Row 2: P2, *k2, p2; rep from * to end.
Rep these 2 rows once more.
Join in A and work 2 rows in st st, dec 1 st at beg of first row (45 sts).

Start pattern

Row 1: Work 4-st rep of chart 1 to last st, work 1 st A.

Row 2: Work first st A, work 4-st rep of chart 1 to end.

Row 3: Work 4-st rep of chart 1 to last st, work 1 st A.

Rows 4–5: Work 2 rows st st in A.

Row 6: Work 1 st in A, (work 12-st rep of chart 2) three times, work last 8 sts of chart 2.

Row 7: Work first 8 sts of chart 2, (work 12-st rep of chart 2) three times, work last st in A.

Rows 8–9: Cont to follow chart 2, as set, until completed.

Nordic charts

4-st repeat

12-st repeat

12-st repeat

■ A 04 Red

□ B 07 Oatmeal

1 square represents 1 stitch and 1 row

Rows 10–11: Work 2 rows st st in A.
Rows 12–14: P1 A, work rows 1 and 3 of 4-st rep chart 1.
Row 13: Work 4 st rep chart 1 row 2 to last st, k1 A.
Rows 15–16: Work 2 rows st st in A.
Row 17: Work first 8 sts of chart 3, (work 12-st rep of chart 3) three times, k1 in A.
Row 18: P1 in A, (work row 2 of 12-st rep of chart 3) three times, work last 8 sts of row 2 of chart 3.
Rows 19–25: Cont to follow chart 3, as set, until completed.
Rows 26–27: Work 2 rows st st in A.
Rows 28–30: As rows 12–14.
Rows 31–32: Work 2 rows st st in A.

Rows 33 and 35: Work 1st 8 sts chart 2, work 12-st rep chart 2, 3 times, K1 in A.
Rows 34 and 36: P1 in A, work 12-st rep chart 2, 3 times, work last 8 sts chart 2.
Rows 37–38: Work 2 rows st st in A.
Rows 39–41: Work as rows 1–3 of chart 1.
Row 42: Purl 1 row in A, inc 1 st at centre of row (46 sts).

Eyelet row
Row 43: K4 (k2tog, yf, k4) seven times.

Rib edging
Row 1: Using A, k2, *p2, k2; rep from * to end.
Row 2: Using A, p2, *k2, p2; rep from * to end.
Rep these 2 rows once more, then row 1 again.
Cast off in B.

Making up
Sew side seams, leaving gap for handle and spout.
Cut 6 strands of yarn 30in (75cm) long, 2 in each colour, and form into a plait. Thread through eyelets.
Cut three 30in (75cm) strands in each of A and B. Make into a plait, and thread through the eyelets.

This cozy is adorned with a friendly nurse and is bound to cheer up the recipient. Why not swap the colours for other yarns to make different characters, or use different accessories?

Get well soon

Materials

Sirdar Hayfield Bonus DK, 100% acrylic
(306yds/280m per 100g ball)
1 x 100g ball in 961 White (A)
1 x 100g ball in 969 Bluebell (B)
1 x 100g ball in 963 Flesh Tone (C)
Sirdar Funky Fur, 100% polyester (98yds/90m per 50g ball)
1 x 50g ball in 548 Chocolate (D)
Oddments of red and black yarn to embroider face
Pair of 3.75mm (UK9:US5) knitting needles
Pair of 4mm (UK8:US6) knitting needles

Spare needle or stitch holder
Toy stuffing
'Watch' button
Red crayon or blusher
Tapestry needle

Tension

22 sts and 28 rows to 4in (10cm) over st st using 3.75mm needles and Sirdar Hayfield Bonus DK. Use larger or smaller needles if necessary to obtain the correct tension.

Body (make 2)

Using 3.75mm needles and B, cast on 42 sts.

Work in g st for 4 rows.

Row 5: Knit.

Row 6: K2, p38, k2.

Rep rows 5–6 three more times.

Change to A and work in g st for 4 rows.

Rep rows 5–6 for 16 rows.

Work in g st for 4 rows.

Change to B and rep rows 5–6 until piece measures 5in (12.5cm) from cast-on edge (or to fit your teapot).

Dec as follows:

Next row: *K5, k2tog; rep from * to end (36 sts).

Next row: Purl.

Next row: *K4, k2tog; rep from * to end (30 sts).

Next row: Purl.

Next row: *K3, k2tog; rep from * to end (24 sts).

Next row: Purl.

Now hold the yarn double to give strength to the neck.

Next row: *K2, k2tog; rep from * to end (18 sts).

Break yarn and leave sts on spare needle or stitch holder.

Work a second piece to match but do not break yarn.

Head

Using B and holding yarn double, purl across both sets of sts (36 sts).

Change to C, holding yarn double, work in st st for 2 rows.

Next row: Now holding yarn single, *k2, inc; rep from * to end (48 sts).

Work in st st for 23 rows.

Next row: K2tog to end (24 sts).

Next row: P2tog to end (12 sts).

Break yarn, leaving a long tail, thread tail through these sts and fasten off securely.

Hair

Using 4mm needles and D, cast on 12 sts.

Row 1: K2tog; k to last 3 sts, turn.

Row 2: K to last st, inc in last st.

Row 3: K to last 2 sts, turn.

Row 4: Knit.

Row 5: K across all sts.

Row 6: Knit.

Rep these 6 rows ten times.

Cast off.

Collar

Using 3.75mm needles and A, cast on 40 sts.

Work in g st for 3 rows.

Next row: *K2, k2tog; rep from * to end (30 sts).

Cast off.

Bow

Using 3.75mm needles and A, cast on 4 sts.

Work in g st for 8in (20cm).

Cast off.

Hat

Using 3.75mm needles and A, cast on 54 sts.

Work in st st for 4 rows.

Cont in st st, cast off 8 sts at beg of next 2 rows (38 sts).

Dec 1 st at each end of next and every foll row until 24 sts rem.

Work in st st for 28 rows.

Work in g st for 2 rows.

Cast off.

Bib

Using 3.75mm needles and A, cast on 12 sts.

Work in g st for 2 rows.

Work in st st for 11 rows.

Work in g st for 2 rows.

Cast off.

Making up

Sew up the sides of the cozy body, leaving room for the handle and spout of the teapot.

Sew up the side of the head.

Stuff and run a gathering thread around the neck, but do not pull too tight.

Embroider the eyes and mouth, using the photograph as a guide.

Pinch in nose and catch with a stitch.

Blush cheeks using red crayon or blusher.

Sew cast-on and cast-off edges of hair together. The wavy set of row ends is the face edge. Gather opposite sets of row ends tightly and fasten. Place onto head and sew in place (attach each point of wave to face with a stitch). Place the collar around the neck and sew the ends together.

Sew the bib in place at front of body (as picture). Attach 'watch' button to one corner.

Join short straight sets of row ends of hat. Place on head with the seam at the back. Stitch into place, onto hair. Fold the hat back and join the cast-off edge and the cast-on edge. Shape as in picture.

Make the garter-stitch strip into a bow and sew onto back of dress, as in photograph.

Weave in all ends.

This is the ultimate cozy to give your tea table some extra-bright shabby chic. It's a great project for using up leftover yarn in any colours, which will give your cozy a thrift-style effect.

Pretty pompom

Materials

Rico Design Essentials Merino DK, 100% wool (131yds/120m per 50g ball)

1 × 50g ball in 010 Magenta (A)

1 × 50g ball in 071 Lobster (B)

1 × 50g ball in 060 Natural (C)

1 × 50g ball in 065 Yellow (D)

1 × 50g ball in 027 Indigo (E)

1 × 50g ball in 042 Green (F)

1 × 50g ball in 005 Red (G)

3.5mm (UK9/USE/4) crochet hook

Tapestry needle

Tension

6.5 tr cluster sts and 13 rows to 4in (10cm) over V shell pattern using 3.5mm hook. Use a larger or smaller hook if necessary to obtain the correct tension.

Special abbreviations

MC: Magic circle (see page 148)

Tea cozy

Round 1: With 3.5mm hook and A, make a MC, work 8dc, sl st in first dc to join (8 sts).

Round 2: 3ch, tr in same st, 2tr into each st, join with sl st (16 sts).

Round 3: Change to B, 3ch, 1tr in same st, 1ch, *2tr in next st, 1ch; rep from * 14 times, sl st in 3rd ch (16 clusters).

Round 4: Change to C, 3ch, 2tr in next ch sp, *3tr in next ch sp; rep from * 14 times, sl st in 3rd ch (16 clusters).

Round 5: Change to D, 3ch, 2tr in sp between clusters, *3tr between clusters; rep from * 14 times, sl st in 3rd ch (16 clusters).

Round 6: Change to E, 3ch, 2tr in sp between clusters, 1ch, *3tr between clusters, 1ch; rep from * 14 times, sl st in 3rd ch (16 clusters).

Round 7: Change to F, 3ch, (1tr, 1ch, 2tr) in next ch sp, *(2tr, 1ch, 2tr) in next ch sp; rep from * 14 times, sl st in 3rd ch (32 clusters).

Round 8: Change to G, 3ch, 2tr in next sp, *3tr in next sp; rep from * 30 times, sl st in 3rd ch (32 clusters). Work now divides for the two sides of the tea cozy.

Side 1

Row 1: Change to A, 3ch, 2tr in sp at base of ch, *3tr in next sp; rep from * 12 times, turn (14 clusters).

Row 2: Change to B, 3ch, *3tr in next sp; rep from * 12 times, 1tr in 3rd ch of previous row, turn (13 clusters).

Row 3: Change to C; rep row 1.

Row 4: Change to D; rep row 2.

Row 5: Change to E; rep row 1.

Row 6: Change to F; rep row 2.

Row 7: Change to G; rep row 1.

Row 8: Change to A; rep row 2.

Row 9: Change to B; rep row 1.

Row 10: Change to C; rep row 2.

Fasten off work at the end of this row.

Side 2

Return to the top of the tea cozy.

Row 1: Change to A, miss three clusters of previous round, join yarn in next sp, 3ch, 2tr in sp at base of ch, *3tr in next sp; rep from * 12 times, turn (14 clusters).

Cont to match the pattern for side 1, working rows 2–10.

Row 11: Change to D, 3ch, 2tr in sp at base of ch, *3tr in next sp; rep from * 12 times, then join to first side of tea cozy by working 3tr into first sp of side 1, *3tr in next ch sp; rep from * 12 times, sl st in 3rd ch (28 clusters).

Cont to work in rounds.

Round 1: Change to E, 3ch, 2tr in sp at base of ch, *3tr in next sp; rep from * 26 times, sl st in 3rd ch (28 clusters).

Round 2: Change to B, 1ch, dc in each tr around, sl st in ch (84 sts).

Round 3: 1ch, dc in each dc around, sl st in ch (84 sts).

Round 4: Change to C, 1ch, dc in each dc around, sl st in ch (84 sts).

Round 5: 1ch, dc in each dc around, sl st in ch (84 sts).

Fasten off and weave in all ends.

Pompom

Make a 2in (5cm) pompom using A (see page 151) and sew firmly to the top of the tea cozy.

This detailed double-sided design has bunting, a teapot, cupcake stand, a multitude of mini cupcakes and a large cupcake to top the ensemble. It would make a perfect gift for a keen baker or a cake lover.

Tea and bunting

Materials

Rico Essentials Cotton DK, 100% mercerized cotton (142yds/130m per 50g ball)
1 x 50g ball in 044 Patina (A)
1 x 50g ball in 051 Natural (B)
1 x 50g ball in 093 Erica (C)
1 x 50g ball in 095 Aqua (D)
1 x 50g ball in 080 White (E)
Small amounts of:
015 Berry (F)

084 Cardinal (G)
040 Dark Teal (H)
019 Dusky (I)
016 Lilac (J)
004 Cherry (K)
Pair of 3.5mm (UK9:US4) knitting needles
Spare needles or stitch holders
Polyester toy stuffing
Tapestry needle

Tension

22 sts and 28 rows to 4in (10cm) over st st using 3.5mm needles. Use larger or smaller needles if necessary to obtain the correct tension.

Body

Using 3.5mm needles and A, cast on 104 sts.

Work in st st for 6 rows.

Next row (picot edging): K1, (yf, k2tog) to the last st, k1.

Work in st st for 6 rows.

Next row: K50, cast off 4 sts (for spout opening), place rem 50 sts on stitch holder.

Work on the first 50 sts only.

***Next row:** Purl.

Work in Fairisle pattern using B and C, following chart on page 81:

Row 1: (K2 B, k2 C) to last 2 sts, k2 B.

Row 2: (P2 B, p2 C) to last 2 sts, p2 B.

Row 3: (K2 C, k2 B) to last 2 sts, k2 C.

Row 4: (P2 C, p2 B) to last 2 sts, p2 C.

Rep the last 4 rows three times.

Change to D.

Work 26 rows in st st. Place sts on a stitch holder.*

Working on 50 sts from other stitch holder, with WS facing work from * to *.

With RS facing, knit 50 sts on needle and 50 sts from stitch holder (100 sts).

Shaping

Row 1 (and every alt row): Purl.
Row 2: (K3, k2tog) to end (80 sts).
Row 4: Knit.
Row 6: (K6, k2tog) to end (70 sts).
Row 8: (K5, k2tog) to end (60 sts).
Row 10: (K4, k2tog) to end (50 sts).
Row 12: (K3, k2tog) to end (40 sts).
Row 14: (K2, k2tog) to end (30 sts).
Row 16: (K1, k2tog) to end (20 sts).
Break yarn, leaving a long tail, thread tail through these sts and fasten off securely.

Turn under picot hem and sew in place. Using your teapot as a guide, sew up both sides leaving enough room for the spout and handle. Pick up sts on both sides of the opening and knit a 2-row border for extra strength.

Bunting (make 10)

Cast on 2 sts using F, G, H, I or J.
Row 1: Purl.
Row 2: Inc in first and last st (4 sts).
Rep last 2 rows until 8 sts are on needle, ending with row 2.
Work in st st for 3 rows.
Leave bunting on needle.
Make next piece of bunting in the same way using a different colour.
Knit across all ten pieces of bunting in C.
Knit 1 row. Cast off.
Sew the bunting to the top of the tea cozy.

Cupcake stand

Using E, cast on 30 sts.
Knit 1 row.
Starting with a knit row, work in st st for 2 rows.
Cast off 13 sts at beg of next 2 rows. Working on rem 4 sts, knit 6 rows in st st.
Cast on 10 sts at beg of next 2 rows.
Cast off 10 sts at beg of next 2 rows.
Work in st st for 6 rows.
Cast on 8 sts at beg of next 2 rows.
Cast off 8 sts at beg of next 2 rows.
Work in st st for 4 rows.
Cast off.
Sew the stand in place with white thread or yarn on the back of the tea cozy.

Mini cupcakes (make 11)

Using your choice of colour, cast on 6 sts.
Next row: Purl.
Next row: Inc in every st (12 sts).
Work in st st for 2 rows.
Next row: Knit.
Change to E.
Next row: Knit.
Next row: Purl.
Next row: K2tog to end (6 sts).
Next row: P2tog to end (3 sts).
Break yarn, leaving a long tail, thread tail through these sts and fasten off securely.
Using the photograph as a guide, sew eight mini cupcakes to the stand.

Tea and Bunting chart

Row 1: K	B	B	C	C	B	B	C	C	B	B
Row 2: P	B	B	C	C	B	B	C	C	B	B
Row 3: K	C	C	B	B	C	C	B	B	C	C
Row 4: P	C	C	B	B	C	C	B	B	C	C

Teapot

Using E, cast on 28 sts.

Knit 2 rows.

Starting with a knit row, work in st st for 15 rows.

Next row: (P1, p2tog) to end (18 sts).

Purl 1 row for lid.

Knit 1 row.

Starting with a knit row, work in st st for 5 rows.

Next row: P2tog to end (9 sts).

Next row: Inc in every st (18 sts).

Break yarn, leaving a long tail, thread tail through these sts and fasten off securely, wrapping around sts to form teapot knob. Fold teapot in half.

Spout

Using E, cast on 12 sts.

Starting with a knit row, work in st st for 5 rows.

Next row: P2, (p2tog) four times, p2 (8 sts).

Work in st st for 4 rows.

Cast off.

Fold in half lengthwise and attach to the teapot on the right-hand side.

Handle

Using E, cast on 20 sts.

Work in st st for 2 rows.

Cast off.

Attach to the teapot on the left-hand side.

Sew the completed teapot to the front of the tea cozy.

Teacup

Using E, cast on 14 sts.

Knit 1 row.

Starting with a knit row, work in st st for 5 rows.

Next row: P2tog to end (7 sts).

Break yarn, leaving a long tail, thread tail through these sts and fasten off securely. Fold teacup in half.

Teacup handle

Using E, cast on 7 sts.

Knit 1 row.

Cast off.

Attach the handle to the teacup.

Saucer

Using E, cast on 20 sts.

Knit 2 rows.

Next row: P2tog to end (10 sts).

Next row: K2tog to end (5 sts)

Break yarn, leaving a long tail, thread tail through these sts and fasten off securely.

Fan out the saucer to form a circle and sew it next to the teapot and sew on the teacup.

Plate

Using E, cast on 26 sts.

Knit 3 rows.

Next row: P2tog to end (13 sts)

Knit 1 row.

Next row: P2tog to last st, p1 (7 sts).

Break yarn, leaving a long tail, thread tail through these sts and fasten off securely.

Fan out the plate to form a circle, sew the plate below the teapot and add three mini cupcakes.

Large cupcake for top

Using C, cast on 6 sts.

Row 1: Purl.

Row 2: Inc in every st (12 sts).

Row 3: Purl.

Row 4: (Inc, k1) to end (18 sts).

Row 5: Purl.

Row 6: (Inc, k1) to end (27 sts).

Row 7: Purl.

Row 8: (Inc, k2) to end (36 sts).

Rows 9–11: Purl.

Row 12: (K2, p1) to end.

Row 13: (K1, p2) to end.

Rep rows 12–13 three more times.

Row 20: (K2, p1) to end.

Row 21: Knit 1 row for ridge.

Change to B.

Rows 22–25: Starting with knit row, work in st st.

Change to E for icing.

Rows 26–27: Work 2 rows in st st.

Row 28: (K5, k2tog) to last st, k1 (31 sts).

Row 29: Purl.

Row 30: (K4, k2tog) to last st, k1 (26 sts).

Row 31: Purl.

Row 32: K2tog to end (13 sts).

Row 33: Purl.

Row 34: K2tog to last st, k1 (7 sts).

Change to J for cherry, leaving a tail of approx 6in (15cm).

Row 35: Purl.

Row 36: Inc to end (14 sts).

Row 37: Purl.

Row 38: Knit.

Row 39: Purl.

Row 40: P2tog to end.

Break yarn, leaving a long tail, thread tail through these sts and fasten off securely.

Making up

Stuff the cupcake and sew up the side seam. Using the other tail of J, wrap yarn around the base of the cherry and fasten off. Weave in all ends. Sew the cupcake to the top of the cozy.

A really special yarn is used to create a design that would make a perfect gift – or why not treat yourself to a touch of teatime luxury? The cozy features a pretty cable pattern that shows off the fine alpaca yarn.

Colourful cables

Materials

Artesano DK 100% superfine alpaca
(100yds/109m per 50g ball)
2 x 50g balls in 1492 Belize
Small amount of contrasting 4-ply yarn for I-cord
Pair of 3.75mm (UK9:US5) knitting needles
Pair of 4mm (UK8:US6) knitting needles
2 x 3mm or 3.25mm double-pointed needles to make I-cord
Cable needle
Tapestry needle

Tension

26 sts measure 4in (10cm) in width over cable pattern using 4mm needles. Use larger or smaller needles if necessary to obtain the correct tension.

Sides (make 2)

Using 3.75mm needles, cast on 52 sts very loosely. Beg with a purl row, work 3 rows in st st.

Next row (picot holes): (K2, yf, k2tog) to last 2 sts, k2.

Work 3 further rows in st st.

Next row: Form picot edge by taking one stitch from row and one stitch from cast-on edge and knitting together. Rep across row.

Cable pattern

Change to 4mm needles.

Row 1: (K2, p8) across row to last 2 sts, k2.

Cable row: (K2, cab4b, cab4f); rep to last 2 sts, k2.

Next row: As row 1.

Next row: Knit across.

Rep last 2 rows once, then row 1 again.

Work as set, cabling every 6th row until 6 cable rows in total have been worked. Adjust length at this point if necessary.

Next row: As row 1.

Next row: (K2tog, k8); rep to last 2 sts, k2tog (46 sts).

Next row: (K1, p8); rep to last st, k1.

Next row: (K2tog, k7); rep to last 10 sts, k2tog, k6, k2tog (40 sts).

Next row: Purl.

Next row: (Cab4b, cab4f) across row.

Next row: Purl.

Next row: (Skpo, k4, k2tog) across row (30 sts).

Next row: Purl.

Next row: (Skpo, k2, k2tog) across row (20 sts).

Next row: Purl.

Next row: (Skpo, k2tog) across row (10 sts).

Next row: Purl.

Next row (eyelets): K2, (yf, k2tog); rep across row.

Next row: Purl.

Next row: Inc in every st (20 sts).

Next row: Purl.

Next row: Knit.

Next row: Purl.

Next row (picot holes): K2, (yf, k2tog); rep to end.

Next row: Beg with a purl row, work in st st for 4 rows.
Cast off, leaving a long end for making up.

I-cord

Using dpns, cast on 3 sts and work for approx 18in (45.5cm).

Making up

Join lower side edges of work for 1in (2.5cm). Join upper side edges for 3in (7.5cm).
Fold back top picot edge and catch in place loosely on inside of work. Do the same to the lower edge if you did not knit together stitches to form the picot. Press the lower picot edge lightly but do not press the cable section. Thread the I-cord through the eyelet holes. If desired, roll the last section of I-cord into a circle shape and catch in place. Weave in all ends.

This is the perfect tea cozy to get you in the festive mood.
The pattern is straightforward, so why not make several
to give as Christmas presents to friends and family?

Plum pudding

Materials

Rico Design Essentials Soft Merino Aran, 100% merino wool
(109yds/100m per 50g ball)

1 x 50g ball in 059 Brown (A)

1 x 50g ball in 061 Cream (B)

Small amount of 008 Red (C)

Small amount of 047 Fir Green (D)

3.5mm (UK9:USE/4) crochet hook

4mm (UK8:USG/6) crochet hook

Small amount of polyester toy stuffing

Dressmaking pins

1 x ½in (1.25cm) button

Co-ordinating sewing thread

Tapestry needle

Tension

18 sts and 22 rows to 4in (10cm) over dc using 4mm hook.
Use a larger or smaller hook if necessary to obtain the
correct tension.

Special abbreviations

MC: Magic circle (see page 148)

Pudding base

Row 1: Using 4mm hook and A, make 65ch.

Row 2: 1dc in 2nd ch from hook, dc into each ch to end, turn (64 sts).

Rows 3–7: 1ch, 1dc into each st to end, turn (64 sts).

Side 1

Row 8 (RS): *1ch, 28dc, turn (28 sts).

Rows 9–26: 1ch, 28dc, turn* (28 sts). Fasten off.

Side 2

With RS facing, miss central 8 sts on row 8, and rejoin yarn; rep from * to *.

Row 27: 1ch, dc across all sts of side 1 and side 2 (56 sts).

Fasten off and weave in ends.

Pudding top

Round 1: With 4mm hook and B make a MC, work 6dc, sl st in first dc to join (6 sts).

Now work in continuous rounds.

Round 2: 2dc into each st, (12 sts).

Round 3: (1dc, work 2dc into next st); rep around (18 sts).

Round 4: (2dc, work 2dc into next st); rep around (24 sts).

Round 5: (3dc, work 2dc into next st); rep around (30 sts).

Round 6: (4dc, work 2dc into next st); rep around (36 sts).

Round 7: (5dc, work 2dc into next st); rep around (42 sts).

Round 8: (6dc, work 2dc into next st); rep around (48 sts).

Round 9: (7dc, work 2dc into next st); rep around (54 sts).

Round 10: (8dc, work 2dc into next st); rep around (60 sts).

Round 11: (9dc, work 2dc into next st); rep around (66 sts).

Round 12: (10dc, work 2dc into next st); rep around (72 sts).

Round 13: (11dc, work 2dc into next st); rep around (78 sts).

Round 14: (12dc, work 2dc into next st); rep around (84 sts).

Do not break yarn.

Shell pattern: *Miss 1dc, 4tr into next st, miss 1dc, sl st into next st; rep from * around the edge of the pudding top, sl st into first st. Fasten off and weave in ends.

Berries (make 2)

Round 1: With 3.5mm hook and C make a MC, work 6dc (6 sts).

Now work in continuous rounds.

Round 2: (1dc, work 2dc into next st); rep around (9 sts).

Rounds 3–4: 1dc in each st; rep around (9 sts).

Round 5: (1dc, dc2tog); rep around (6 sts).

Stuff the centre of the berry with a little polyester toy stuffing. Thread yarn through rem sts and pull up. Fasten off.

Holly leaves (make 2)

Row 1: With 3.5mm hook and D, make 16ch.

Row 2: 1htr in 3rd ch from hook, htr into each ch to end, turn (14 sts). 3ch, sl st in st at base of ch, *1 sl st in next st, 1dc in next st, 3ch, sl st in same st; rep from * to last st, sl st in last st (7 picots).

Fasten off and leave a long tail of yarn. Fold the leaf in half and sew the central ch sts together.

Buttonhole

Using 3.5mm hook and A, rejoin yarn to the edge of the left side of the pudding base where the cozy opens for the handle, 5ch, miss 2 rows, sl st into next row, turn, work 7dc into ch loop, sl st at base of chain. Fasten off and weave in ends.

Making up

Pin the top of the pudding to the pudding bottom. Using B, whip stitch (see page 150) the circumference of the pudding top to the inside of the pudding bottom.

Using matching sewing thread, sew the holly leaves and the berry to the top of the pudding. Sew a button on the right-hand side of the cozy to correspond to the buttonhole.

This beautiful design is worked in the traditional colours of a rose-filled country garden. The motif on the cozy is worked using the intarsia method (see page 144), while 3D roses are sewn around the bottom of the cozy.

Rose garden

Materials

Rico Essentials Soft Merino Aran, 100% merino wool
(109yds/100m per 50g ball)
1 × 50g ball in 61 Cream (A)
1 × 50g ball in 15 Fuchsia (B)
1 × 50g ball in 12 Orchid (C)
1 × 50g ball in 50 Pistachio (D)
Debbie Bliss Cashmerino Aran, 55% merino, 33% microfibre,
12% cashmere (98yds/90m per 50g ball)
1 × 50g ball in 34 Gold (E)

Pair of 5mm (UK6:US8) knitting needles
Pair of 4mm (UK8:US6) knitting needles
Tapestry needle

Tension

18 sts and 24 rows to 4in (10cm) over st st using 5mm needles and Rico Essentials Soft Merino Aran. Use larger or smaller needles if necessary to obtain the correct tension.

Sides (make 2)

With 5mm needles and A, cast on 44 sts and knit 1 row.

Beg with a knit row, work 12 rows in st st.

Beg motif:

Row 1: K8 A, work 28 sts chart row 1, k8 A.

Row 2: P8 A, work 28 sts chart row 2, p8 A.

Cont to follow chart until 19 rows of motif have been worked.

Beg with a p row, work 11 rows st st in A.

Eyelet row: K3 (k2tog, yf, k4) six times, k2tog, yf, k3.

Using A, work 5 rows in g st.

Join in E and work 2 rows in g st.

Cast off with E.

Roses (make 6 each in B and C)

With 4mm needles and B or C, cast on 73 sts.

Row 1: K1, *k2, pass first st over 2nd st; rep from * to end (37 sts).

Row 2: P2tog to last st, p1 (19 sts).

Row 3: K1, (k2tog) to end (10 sts).

Row 4: P2tog to end (5 sts).

Break off yarn, leaving approx 8in (20cm) and draw through rem sts. Fasten off and leave rem yarn for sewing.

Rosebuds (make 1 each in B and C)

Using 4mm needles and B or C, cast on 5 sts.

Row 1: K, inc in every st (10 sts).

Row 2: Purl.

Row 3: (K1, M1) nine times, k1 (19 sts).

Rows 4–6: Work in st st.

Cast off.

Roll sideways and sew row ends to secure.

Making up

Sew side seams, leaving a gap for the handle and spout.

Pin the roses along lower edges, six on each side, alternating colours, and sew in place.

Cut two × 30in (75cm) strands of B, C and E, and make into a plait. Thread through eyelets, and sew a rosebud to each end of the tie.

Weave in all ends.

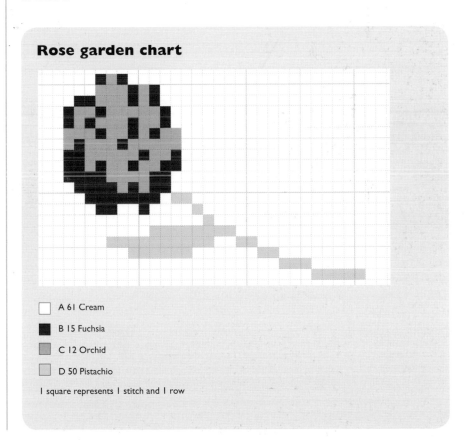

Rose garden chart

☐ A 61 Cream

■ B 15 Fuchsia

▦ C 12 Orchid

▨ D 50 Pistachio

1 square represents 1 stitch and 1 row

Despite its profusion of extravagant bobbles, this is actually
a straightforward design to make for an average-sized teapot,
intended to cover the handle and spout.

Bobble madness

Materials

Sirdar Bonus DK, 100% acrylic (306yds/280m per 100g ball)

1 × 100g ball in 965 Black (A)

1 × 100g ball in 884 Neon (B)

Pair of 4mm (UK8:US6) knitting needles

Tapestry needle

Tension

22 sts and 28 rows to 4in (10cm) over st st using 4mm
needles. Use larger or smaller needles if necessary to obtain
the correct tension.

Sides (make 2)

Using 4mm needles and A, cast on 42 sts.

Row 1: P2, k to last 2 sts, p2.

Row 2: Purl.

Change colours before and after each bobble. Bobbles are made in B.

Row 3: P2, k2, MB, (k4, MB) to last 2 sts, p2.

Row 4: Purl.

Row 5: P2, MB, (k4, MB) to last 4 sts, k2, p2.

Row 6: Purl.

Repeat rows 3–6 until work measures 10in (25cm).

Cast off.

Rim

Cast on 6 sts in B.

Change colours before and after each bobble. Bobbles are made in A.

Row 1: K2, (MB), K3.

Row 2: Purl.

Row 3: K3, (MB), K2.

Row 4: Purl.

Cont until work is long enough to attach up the sides and across the top.

Cast off.

Making up

Sew the two sides together. Weave in all ends.

Special abbreviations

MB: Make bobble – k1, p1, k1, p1 into next st, turn p4, turn k4, turn p4, turn k4tog tbl

This design combines the gathered columns of a traditional cozy with the effect of a jester's hat. Worked in chunky yarn, it is quick to make and extra warm. The stripes are made using a stranding technique.

Jester lovely cuppa

Materials

James C Brett Chunky with Merino, 70% acrylic, 20% polyamide, 10% wool (164yds/150m per 100g ball)

1 × 100g ball in CM4 (A)

1 × 100g ball in CM13 (B)

Pair of 4mm (UK8:US6) knitting needles

Pair of 5mm (UK6:US8) knitting needles

Spare needle or stitch holder

Tapestry needle

Tension

Approx 13 sts to 4in (10cm) over st st using 5mm needles. Only width is crucial. Use larger or smaller needles if necessary to obtain the correct tension. Each side should measure approximately 8½in (21.5cm) across the reverse of the work; if your work measures less you are probably pulling the yarn too tightly across at the colour changes.

Side 2

Using 4mm needles and A, cast on 74
sts loosely and work 2 rows in g st.
Change to 5mm needles, join in B and
strand the yarn tightly across back of
work. Knit the first and last stitch of
every row using a strand of each
colour of yarn to form a firm edge.

Row 1: K1 using both colours, *(k8 A,
k8 B); rep from * to last 9 sts, k8A, k1
using both colours.

Row 2: K1 using both colours, *(p8 A,
p8 B); rep from * to last 9 sts, p8A, k1
using both colours.

Rep last 2 rows until work measures
5½in (14cm) ending with a WS row.

Next row: K1 using both colours,
changing yarn appropriately (k2tog tbl,
k4, k2tog); rep to last st, k1 using both
colours (56 sts).

Next row: K1 using both colours,
changing colours appropriately and
stranding yarn as before, p to last st, k1
using both colours.

Next row: Knit across, changing yarn
appropriately.

Next row: K1 using both colours,
changing colours appropriately and
stranding yarn as before, p to last st, k1
using both colours.

Next row: K2, p to last 2 sts, k2.

Next row: K1 using both colours,
changing yarn appropriately (k2tog tbl,
k2, k2tog); rep to last st, k1 using both
colours (38 sts).

Next row: K1 using both colours,
changing colours appropriately and
stranding yarn as before, p to last st, k1
using both colours.

Next row: Knit across, changing yarn
appropriately.

Next row: K1 using both colours,
changing colours appropriately and
stranding yarn as before, p to last st, k1
using both colours.

Next row: K2, p to last 2 sts, k2.

Next row: K1 using both colours,
changing yarn appropriately (k2tog tbl,
k2tog); rep to last st, k1 using both
colours (20 sts).

Next row: K1 using both colours,
changing colours appropriately and
stranding yarn as before, p to last st, k1
using both colours.

Break off yarn, leaving a long end for
sewing up. Leave sts on a spare needle
or stitch holder.

Side 1

Work as side 2, but only break off
contrast yarn at end.
Cont in A only, working the two
strands of the first and last st, using
one strand of A.

Join sides

Next row: K1, (k2tog) nine times,
place set-aside sts on needle and k2tog
across join, (k2tog) nine times, k1
(21 sts).

Next row (eyelets): K1, (yf, k2tog);
rep to end (21 sts).

Next row: K1, inc in each st to last st,
k1 (40 sts).

Knit 2 rows, ending with WS facing
ready to work triangles. Note that for
these, st st should be uppermost when
they flip over.

Make triangles

Row 1: Inc in first st, p8, inc in next st,
turn (12 sts).

Row 2 and foll even rows: Knit
across.

Row 3: K1, p10, k1.

Row 5: K1, p2tog, p6, p2tog tbl, k1
(10 sts).

Row 7: K1, p8, k1.

Row 9: K1, p2tog, p4, p2tog tbl, k1
(8 sts).

Row 11: K1, p6, k1.

Row 13: K1, p2tog, p2, p2tog tbl, k1
(6 sts).

Row 15: K1, p4, k1.

Row 17: K1, p2tog, p2tog tbl, k1 (4 sts).

Row 19: K1, p2tog, k1 (3 sts).

Row 21: P3tog.

Fasten off, leaving a long end.

Join in B, and moving on to next 10 sts, work another triangle in exactly the same way. Rep with A to work third triangle, then with B for final triangle.

Making up

Join lower edge of cozy for approx 1in (2.5cm). Try cozy on pot and join top edges using mattress stitch (see page 149).

Weave in all ends.

Cut three x 24in (61cm) lengths of yarn and plait to form a tie. Thread through eyelets and tie in a bow.

Make four small pompoms (two of each colour; see page 151) and attach to ends of triangles as shown, using an A pompom on a B triangle and vice versa. Note that it is not necessary to press the work.

This tea cozy, with its delicate sugared-almond colours, has bags of vintage charm. You can alter the shades of the granny square motif to complement your best china.

Granny squares

Materials

Rico Design Essentials Merino DK, 100% merino wool (131yds/120m per 50g ball)

1 x 50g ball in 023 Grey Blue (A)

1 x 50g ball in 020 Mauve (B)

1 x 50g ball in 063 Light Yellow (C)

1 x 50g ball in 001 Rose (D)

1 x 50g ball in 098 Silver Grey (E)

3mm (UK11:US–) crochet hook

20in (50cm) x 10mm ribbon

Tapestry needle

Tension

Each granny square motif measures 1¾in x 1¾in (4.5cm x 4.5cm) using 3mm hook. Use a larger or smaller hook if necessary to obtain the correct tension.

Main granny square motif (make 24)

Round 1: With 3mm hook and B, make 4ch, work 11tr in 4th ch from hook, sl st in top of 3rd ch (counts as 12tr). (See diagram, page 105.)

Round 2: 1htr in same st where sl st was made, work 1htr in each of the next 2 sts, 1ch (1htr in next 3 sts, 1ch) rep twice, join with sl st to top of first htr.

Round 3: Change to A and join yarn in 1ch corner sp, 3ch, work 4tr in same sp, 1ch, 5tr in same sp (5tr in the next corner ch sp, 1ch, 5tr in same sp) rep twice, join with sl st to top of 3ch.
Fasten off and weave in ends.
Work a further five squares that have yarn B at their centre.
Work six squares each using C, D and E for rounds 1–2 and A for round 3.
In total you will need 24 granny squares.

Making up

Using 3mm hook and A, use photographs as a guide and sl st 12 square motifs together for each side. Using 3mm hook and A, attach yarn to any stitch on the edge with a sl st, 1ch, work 1dc in each tr and ch around, working 3dc at each corner so that you have worked evenly around the four edges of each side, sl st into ch.

Bottom edge

With WS together using 3mm hook and A, attach yarn to any stitch on the bottom edge with a sl st, 1ch, work 1dc in each dc around, joining both sides of the tea cozy together, sl st into ch. Work a further 2 rows in dc. Fasten off and weave in ends.

Tea cozy top

Round 1: With WS together using 3mm hook and A, attach yarn to any stitch on the top edge with a sl st, 1ch, work 1dc in each dc around, joining both sides of the tea cozy together, sl st into ch (90 sts).

Round 2: 1ch, dc in each st to end, sl st into ch.

Round 3: 3ch, *3tr, tr2tog; rep from * around, sl st into 3rd ch (72 sts).

Round 4: 3ch, *2tr, tr2tog; rep from * around, sl st into 3rd ch (54 sts).

Round 5: 3ch, *1tr, tr2tog; rep from * around, sl st into 3rd ch (36 sts).

Round 6: 3ch, *tr2tog; rep from * around, sl st into 3rd ch (18 sts).

Round 7: 3ch, 1tr into each st, sl st into 3rd ch (18 sts).

Round 8: 3ch, *2tr in next st; rep from * around, sl st into 3rd ch (36 sts).

Round 9: 3ch, *2tr in next st, 1tr; rep from * around, sl st into 3rd ch (54 sts).

Round 10: 3ch, work 4tr in same st at base of ch, 1ch, 5tr in same sp, * miss 3 sts, (5tr, 1ch, 5tr) in next st; rep from * around, sl st in 3rd ch (13 shell clusters). Fasten off and weave in ends.

Use the tapestry needle to weave the ribbon through stitches in round 7. Pull the ribbon tight and tie in a bow.

Granny square motif

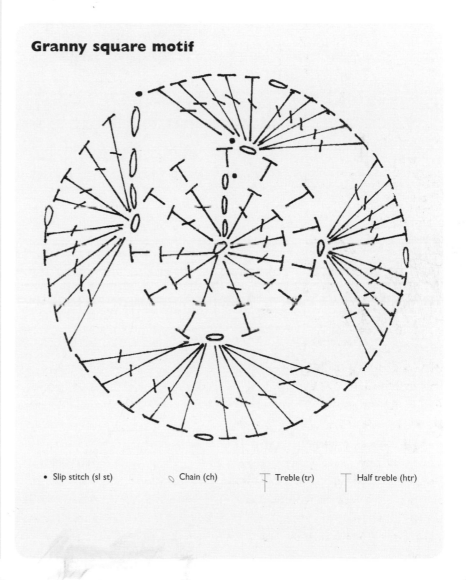

- • Slip stitch (sl st)   ○ Chain (ch)   ⊤ Treble (tr)   ⊤ Half treble (htr)

The dark background colour of this design serves as the perfect canvas to highlight the pansy motifs, which are worked using the intarsia technique. Made in aran-weight wool, this chunky cozy will be well insulated.

Pansies

Materials

Rico Essentials Soft Merino Aran, 100% merino wool
(109yds/100m per 50g ball)
1 x 50g ball in 90 Black (A)
1 x 50g ball in 15 Fuchsia (B)
1 x 50g ball in 12 Orchid (C)
1 x 50g ball in 61 Cream (D)
Debbie Bliss Cashmerino Aran, 55% merino, 33% microfibre,
12% cashmere (98yds/90m per 50g ball)
1 x 50g ball in 34 Gold (E)
1 X 50g ball in 50 Pistachio (F)

Pair of 5mm (UK6:US8) knitting needles
Pair of 3mm (UK11:US–) knitting needles
Spare needle or stitch holder
Embroidery thread in co-ordinating colour
Tapestry needle

Tension

18 sts and 24 rows to 4in (10cm) over st st using 5mm needles and Rico Essentials Soft Merino Aran. Use larger or smaller needles if necessary to obtain the correct tension.

Sides (make 2)

Using 5mm needles and B, cast on 43 sts.
Work 5 rows in g st.
Break off yarn and join in A.
Follow 44 rows of chart, shaping as shown on chart.
Cast off.

Pansies (make 3)

Top front petals (2 per flower)
Using 3mm needles and C, cast on 5 sts.
Row 1: Knit.
Row 2: P1, M1, p3, M1, p1 (7 sts).
Row 3: K1, M1, k5, M1, k1 (9 sts).
Row 4: Purl.

Row 5: K4 C, k1 B, k4 C.
Row 6: P3 C, p3 B, p3 C.
Row 7: K2 C, k5 B, k2 C.
Row 8: P2tog C, p1 C, p3 B, p1 C, p2tog tbl C. (7 sts).
Row 9: Skpo C, k3 B, k2tog C. (5 sts).
Row 10: P2tog C, p1 B, p2tog tbl C. (3 sts).

Leave sts on spare needle or on stitch holder.

Lower front petal (1 per flower)

Using 3mm needles and C, cast on 7 sts.
Row 1: Knit.
Row 2: P1, M1, p5, M1, p1 (9 sts).
Row 3: K1, M1, k7, M1, k1 (11 sts).
Row 4: P3 C, p5 B, p3 C.
Row 5: K2 C, k7 B, k2 C.
Row 6: P2tog C, p1 C, p5 B, p1 C, p2tog tbl C (9 sts).
Row 7: Skpo C, k1 C, k3 B, k1 C, k2tog C (7 sts).
Row 8: P2tog C, p1 C, p1 B, p1 C, p2tog tbl C (5 sts).
Row 9: Skpo C, k1 B, k2tog C (3 sts).
Leave sts on spare needle or on stitch holder.

Top back petals (make 6)

With 3mm needles and B, cast on 5 sts.
Row 1: Knit.
Row 2: P1, M1, p3, M1, p1 (7 sts).
Row 3: K1, M1, k5, M1, k1 (9 sts).
Rows 4 and 6: Purl.
Rows 5 and 7: Knit.
Row 8: P2tog, p5, p2tog tbl (7 sts).
Row 9: Skpo, k3, k2tog (5 sts).
Row 10: P2tog, p1, p2tog tbl. (3 sts).
Leave sts on spare needle or on stitch holder.

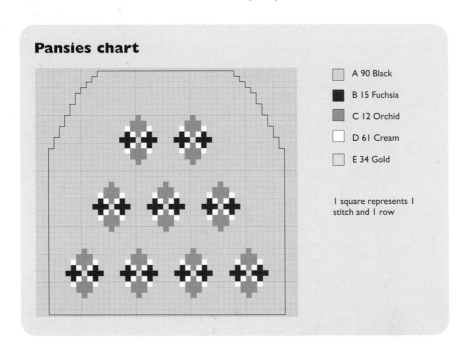

Pansies chart

A 90 Black
B 15 Fuchsia
C 12 Orchid
D 61 Cream
E 34 Gold

1 square represents 1 stitch and 1 row

Leaves (make 3)

With 3mm needles and F, cast on 3 sts.

Foundation row: K1, p1, k1.

Row 1: K1, M1, k1, M1, k1 (5 sts).

Row 2: K2, p1, k2.

Row 3: K2, M1, k1, M1, k2 (7 sts).

Row 4 and foll even rows: K to centre st, p1, k to end.

Rows 5, 7 and 9: Knit.

Row 11: Skpo, k3, k2tog (5 sts).

Row 13: Skpo, k1, k2tog (3 sts).

Row 15: Sl 1, k2tog, psso, fasten off.

Making up

Using a length of embroidery thread and a tapestry needle, thread through the stitches of the two top front petals and one lower front petal left on a stitch holder, repeat once more, pull yarn together tightly, secure, do not fasten off.

With the two top back petals, thread through stitches left on holder, repeat once more, pull the yarn together, secure, place behind the top front petals overlapping them slightly, sew in place.

Using E, embroider French knots (see page 152) at centre of flowers.

Sew sides and top of main pieces, leaving gaps for the handle and spout. Sew pansies onto top centre, sewing leaves underneath flowers. Weave in all ends.

This jolly tea cozy with a garter-stitch striped body features brightly coloured flags that are neatly attached as you knit around the top. The bobble on top completes the circus look.

Big top

Materials

Rowan Pure Wool DK, 100% wool
(136yds/125m per 50g ball)
1 x 50g ball in 036 Kiss (A)
1 x 50g ball in 013 Enamel (B)
1 x 50g ball in 051 Gold (C)
1 x 50g ball in 019 Avocado (D)
Pair of 4mm (UK8:US6) knitting needles
Spare needle or stitch holder
Dressmaking pins
Tapestry needle

Tension

20 sts and 38 rows to 4in (10cm) over g st using 4mm needles. Note that achieving accurate tension is not crucial for this project as the garter-stitch fabric will stretch to fit.

Pattern note

Do not cut ends – carry the yarn up the side of the work, twisting the colours together.

Body (make 2 pieces)

Using 4mm needles and A, cast on 22 sts.

Rows 1–8: Using A, knit.

Rows 9–16: Using B, knit.

Repeat these 16 rows three times more. Cast off.

Flags (make 4 pieces in C and 4 in D)

Cast on 2 sts.

Row 1: Knit.

Row 2: Inc in each st (4 sts).

Row 3: Knit.

Row 4: Inc in first st, knit to last st, inc in last st (6 sts).

Knit 3 rows.

Inc in first st, knit to last st, inc in last st (8 sts).

Knit 4 rows.

Cut yarn and leave flag on a spare needle or stitch holder.

Top

Turn the body pieces round so that the stripes run vertically. Make sure that the top edge is the one with the loops where the second colour is carried up the work.

With RS facing and B, pick up and knit 4 sts from each vertical stripe (64 sts).

Next row: Purl.

Add flags as follows using B:

Insert needle into first st of flag in C and knit it together with first st of main body. Cont in this way until all sts of first flag are attached to main body. Rep with flag in D and keep adding flags (one in C and one in D) until all flags are attached.

Next row: Knit.

Next row: *(K11, k2tog); rep from * to end of row (60 sts).

Next row: Knit.

Next row: *(K4, k2tog); rep from * to end of row (50 sts).

Next row: Purl.

Next row: Knit.

Next row: Purl.

Next row: Change to C, *(k3, k2tog); rep from * to end of row (40 sts).

Next row: Purl.

Next row: *(K2, k2tog); rep from * to end of row (30 sts).

Next row: Purl.

Next row: Change to B, *(k1, k2tog); rep from * to end of row (20 sts).

Next row: Purl.

Next row: K2tog to end of row (10 sts).

Next row: Purl.

Cut yarn and thread tail through rem 10 sts, pulling up tightly.

Fasten off.

Bobble

With A, cast on 1 st leaving a 6in (15cm) yarn tail.

Row 1: Knit into front, back and front of st (3 sts).

Row 2: Knit.

Row 3: Inc in first st, k1, inc in last st (5 sts).

Row 4: Knit.

Row 5: K2tog, k1, k2tog (3 sts).

Row 6: Knit.

Row 7: Sl1, k2tog, psso (1 st).

Cut yarn leaving a 6in (15cm) tail and draw through rem st to fasten off.

Tie the two yarn tails together to draw bobble into shape and fasten with a few sts.

Making up

Sew up crown of tea cozy. Join sides together at bottom with a short seam. This is easier if you put the tea cozy on your teapot and mark the seams with pins.

Cut 15 pieces of yarn approx 5in (12.5cm) long in colours C and D. Take three pieces of yarn and use them to create contrasting tassels at the bottom of the flags using the photograph as a guide.

Sew the bobble to the top of the tea cozy.

This eye-catching intarsia design suits teapots of varying sizes or non-standard shapes – it just drops over the whole pot. The felted fabric is thick and warm, and the felting process is easy to achieve in a washing machine.

Felted diamonds

Materials

Schachenmayr Wash+Filz-it!, 100% wool
(54yds/50m per 50g ball) or Twilleys Freedom,
100% wool (54yds/50m per 50g ball)
3 x 50g balls in Mauve (A)
2 x 50g balls in Black (B)
Pair of 6.5mm (UK3:US10.5) knitting needles
Spare needle or stitch holder
Tapestry needle

Tension

Achieving accurate tension is not crucial for this project as the work will shrink when felted and can be pulled to the required size.

Pattern note

If the cozy is larger than you want after the first wash, simply repeat the felting process to reduce the size. The diamond pattern is achieved using the intarsia colourwork technique (see page 144).

Side 1

Using 6.5mm needles and B, cast on 50 sts loosely.

*Work 6 rows in st st.

Next row: K tog 1 st from working row and 1 st from cast-on edge to make hem.*

Next row: Join in A and p across 50 sts on needle.

Work in st st for a further 11 rows in A, ending with WS facing to begin pattern.

Pattern

Row 1: P6A, (p2 B, p10 A); rep to last 8 sts, p2 B, p6 A.

Row 2: K5A, (k4 B, k8 A); rep to last 9 sts, k4 B, k5 A.

Row 3: P4 A, (p6 B, p6 A); rep to last 10 sts, p6 B, p4 A.

Row 4: K3 A, (k8 B, k4 A); rep to last 11 sts, k8 B, k3 A.

Row 5: P2 A; (p4 B, p2 A); rep to end.

Row 6: K1 A, k4 B, (k4 A, k8 B); rep to last 9 sts, k4 A, k4 B, k1 A.

Row 7: (P2 A, p4 B); rep to last 2 sts, p2 A.

Row 8: K3 A, (k8 B, k4 A); rep to last 11 sts, k8 B, k3 A.

Row 9: P4 A, (p6 B, p6 A); rep to last 10 sts, p6 B, p4 A.

Row 10: K5 A, (k4 B, k8 A); rep to last 9 sts, k4 B, k5 A.

Row 11: P6 A, (p2 B, p10 A); rep to last 8 sts, p2 B, p6 A.

Beg with a k row, work in st st until piece measures 8½in (21.5cm) from hem (8 rows).

Shape top

Dec 1 st at beg and end of next and every foll alt row until 40 sts rem. Dec 1 st at beg and end of every row until 20 sts rem. Cast off loosely.

Side 2

Cast on 56 sts and work as for side 1 from * to *.

Next row: Place first 6 sts on a spare needle or stitch holder but do not break off B. Join in A and purl across rem 50 sts. Working on these 50 sts, complete side 2 to match side 1. Return to 6 sts on holder and work in g st, slipping first st of every row, until strip is long enough to reach all the way round the side of the cozy to the beg of the contrast hem, ending with RS facing.

Next: Work 6 rows in st st for hem. Cast off loosely.

Making up

Pin contrast strip in place all round edges of cozy and attach from RS using mattress stitch (see page 149). Join in hem of contrast strip, matching carefully, and turn last section to WS of work. Weave in all ends.

Felting

Place completed cozy in the drum of a washing machine with an old towel or a pair of jeans to provide the friction necessary to achieve felting. Add a tiny amount of detergent and run through a complete 100°F (40°C) cycle. Remove and pull to shape. Allow to dry naturally. If cozy is too large, repeat the process.

This fanciful autumn-inspired design in a jolly pumpkin orange
with a tendril detail is the perfect tea cozy with which to
celebrate the mellow fruitfulness of the harvest.

Pumpkin

Materials

Rico Design Essentials Soft Merino Aran, 100% merino wool
(109yds/100m per 50g ball)
1 ball 070 in Mandarin (A)
1 ball 050 in Pistachio (B)
4mm (UK8:USG/6) crochet hook
3.5mm (UK9/USE/4) crochet hook
1 x ½in (1.25cm) button
Tapestry needle

Tension

20 sts and 13 rows to 4in (10cm) in htr blo (back loop only)
using 4mm hook. Use a larger or smaller hook if necessary to
obtain the correct tension.

Pumpkin

Row 1: Using 4mm hook and A, make 28ch.

Row 2: 1htr in 3rd ch from hook, htr into each ch to end, turn (26 sts). Work all sts now blo to create rib effect.

Rows 3–22: 2ch, 1htr blo into each st to end, turn (26 sts).

Row 23: 2ch, 1htr blo into next 6 sts, turn (6 sts).

Row 24: 2ch, 6htr blo, turn (6 sts).

Row 25: 2ch, 6htr blo, 16ch, then sl st in last 4 sts of row 22, turn (26 sts).

Row 26: 2ch, 1htr in 4 sl sts and then 1htr in each ch st, 1htr blo in 6 sts of previous row, turn (26 sts).

Rows 27–46: 2ch, 1htr blo into each st to end, turn (26 sts).

Without breaking off yarn, you will now work along the top of the cozy to gather the top together.

Round 1: 3ch, tr2tog in 48 sts evenly around the top of the cozy, approx 2 sts between each rib, sl st in 3rd ch to close (24 sts).

Round 2: 3ch, tr into each st around, sl st in 3rd ch (24 sts).

Round 3: 3ch, *tr2tog, rep from * around, sl st in 3rd ch (12 sts).

Round 4: Change to B and using 3.5mm hook, 1ch, dc in each st around, sl st in ch (12 sts).

Cont in a continuous spiral, dc in each st until stalk measures 1¼in (3.5cm).

Next round: Dc2tog around (6 sts). Cut the yarn and using a tapestry needle weave through the final 6 sts, draw up the yarn and close the hole. Fasten off and weave in ends.

Tendril

Row 1: Using 3.5mm hook and B, make 65ch.

Row 2: 1dc in 2nd ch from hook, dc into each ch to end, turn (64 sts).

Row 3: 1ch, *dc3tog; rep from * to end.

This will create a natural spiral. Fasten off and weave in ends.

Buttonhole

Using 3.5mm hook and A, rejoin yarn to the edge of the left side of the pumpkin where the cozy opens for the handle, 5ch, miss 2 sts, sl st into next st, turn, work 7dc into ch loop, sl st at base of chain. Fasten off and weave in ends.

Making up

Using B, sew tendril securely to the base of the stalk. Using A, sew the top four stitches together at the top of the handle opening.
Sew a button on the right-hand side of the cozy to correspond to the buttonhole.

This elegant tea cozy in traditional colours features crocheted flowers and knitted leaves, which are felted to produce a stunning effect. The addition of retro buttons lends the whole piece a vintage feel.

Vintage roses

Materials

Wendy Supreme Luxury Cotton DK, 100% mercerized cotton (219yds/201m per 100g ball)

2 × 100g balls in 1851 Cream (A)

Woolyknit DK Classics, 100% merino wool (106yds/96m per 50g ball)

1 × 50g ball in Red (B)

Woolyknit Aran, 100% wool (85yds/77m per 50g ball)

1 × 50g ball in Apple (C)

Pair of 4.5mm (UK7:US7) knitting needles

4mm (UK8:USG/6) crochet hook

Spare needle or stitch holder

3 × vintage or retro-style buttons

Tapestry needle

Tension

19 sts and 23 rows to 4in (10cm) over main pattern using Wendy Supreme Luxury Cotton DK yarn double and 4.5mm needles. Use larger or smaller needles to obtain the correct tension.

Pattern notes

Note the body and lining are made with the yarn held double. Once the flowers are crocheted and the leaves knitted they are placed in a net bag, washing bag or pillowcase and then felted in a washing machine at 100–120°F (40–50°C), depending on your machine. It is advisable to test a sample first to achieve the best results. If the pieces do not felt enough the first time, put them back in, maybe at a higher temperature.

Body and lining (make 2)

Using 4.5mm needles and double strand of A, cast on 37 sts.

Row 1: P1, *k1 tbl, p1; rep from * to last st, p1.

Row 2: Knit.

These 2 rows form pattern.

Rep rows 1 and 2 a further 18 times, ending with row 2 and RS facing for next row. Transfer these sts to a spare needle or stitch holder.

Work second side of cozy the same, then place both side by side and work joining row.

Joining row: Work 36 sts in pattern across first piece then purl last st and first st on second piece together, cont in patt to end of row (73 sts).

Shape top

Row 1: P1, *skpo; rep from * to end (37 sts).

Row 2: Knit.

Rep these 2 rows three times more until 6 sts rem. Break yarn, leaving a long tail, thread tail through these sts and fasten off securely.

Work the lining of tea cozy in the same way.

Roses (make 3)

Using 4mm crochet hook and B, leave a long tail and make 48ch.

Row 1: Miss 4ch, 1tr in each of next 3ch, 1dtr in each of next 41ch, turn.

Row 2: 3ch, 3dtr in each of next 41 sts, 3tr in each of rem sts, fasten off.

Using long end of yarn at start of first row, form rose by coiling chain edge anti-clockwise, catch together at back of rose with a tapestry needle as you go.

Sew in ends, then place in a net bag, washing bag or pillowcase and felt in a washing machine at 100–120°F (40–50°C).

Leaves (make 6)

Using 4.5mm needles and C, cast on 3 sts.

Row 1 (RS): Knit.

Row 2: Inc, inc, k1 (5 sts).

Row 3: K2, yf, sl1 p-wise, yb, k2.

Row 4: K1, inc twice, k2 (7 sts).

Row 5 and every odd row: K to centre st, yf, sl 1 p-wise, yb, k to end.

Row 6: K2, inc twice, k3 (9 sts).

Row 8: K3, inc twice, k4 (11 sts).

Row 10: K4, inc twice, k5 (13 sts).

Row 12: K5, inc twice, K6 (15 sts).

Work 7 rows in st st.

Row 20: K1, skpo, k9, k2tog, k1 (13 sts).

Row 22: k1, skpo, k7, k2tog, k1 (11 sts).

Row 24: K1, skpo, k5, k2tog, k1 (9 sts).

Row 26: K1, skpo, k3, k2tog, k1 (7 sts).

Row 28: K1, skpo, k1, k2tog, k1 (5 sts).

Row 30: K1, sl2, k1, p2sso, k1 (3 sts).

Row 32: K3tog, fasten off.

Sew in ends, place in a net bag and felt in washing machine at 100–120°F (40–50°C).

Making up

Join the side seams of the tea cozy and lining, leaving an opening for the handle and for the spout.

Attach the leaves around the top of the tea cozy with the cast-on edges together in the centre.

Sew a button into the centre of each rose, then arrange and attach the roses as shown in the photograph.

Finally, place the lining into the tea cozy with wrong sides facing and slip stitch around the handle and spout openings and around the hem.

Tip

Place the cozy over a teapot to aid you when arranging and attaching the leaves and flowers to the top.

This gloriously eccentric tea cozy with a knitted lining in autumnal green recreates a glossy conker in knitted form. The tweedy yarn lends the piece an authentically rustic air.

Bonkers conker

Materials

Stylecraft Extra Special DK, 100% acrylic
(322yds/294m per 100g ball)
1 x 100g ball in 1124 Greengage (A)
Small amount of white (B) and brown (C) DK yarn
White, or any other colour, DK for lining (D)
Pair of 3.5mm (UK9:US4) knitting needles
4 x stitch markers
Tapestry needle

Tension

22 sts and 30 rows to 4in (10cm) over st st using 3.5mm needles. Use larger or smaller needles if necessary to obtain the correct tension.

Special abbreviations

W&T: Wrap and turn: bring yarn to front; slip next stitch knitwise, turn. Place slipped stitch back on right needle. On subsequent rows, knit the loop along with the slipped stitch

Conker case (make 2)

Using 3.5mm needles and A, cast on 49 sts.

Beg with a k row, work 7 rows in st st.

Row 8: Knit (fold along this row for the hem when making up).

Row 9: Knit.

Row 10 (set-up row): P6, pm, (p12, pm) three times, p7.

Row 11: K6, M1, k1, M1, sm, (k11, M1, k1, M1, sm) three times, k6 (57 sts).

Row 12 and alt rows unless specified: Purl.

Row 13: K6, M1, k3, M1, sm, (k11, M1, k3, M1, sm) three times, k6 (65 sts).

Row 15: K6, M1, k5, M1, sm, (k11, M1, k5, M1, sm) three times, k6 (73 sts).

Row 16: (this row is like a picot edge and creates the sticking-out spikes) P6 (sm, p3, cast on 4 sts in next st and cast them off immediately, p14) three times, sm, p3, cast on 4 sts and cast them off immediately, p9.

Row 17: K6, ssk, k3, k2tog, sm, (k11, ssk, k3, k2tog, sm) three times, k6 (65 sts).

Row 19: K6, ssk, k1, k2tog, sm, (k11, ssk, k1, k2tog, sm) three times, k6 (57 sts).

Row 21: K6, s1, k2tog, psso, sm, (k11, s1, k2tog, psso, sm) three times, k6 (49 sts).

Row 22 (reposition markers for next set of spikes): (P12, pm) three times, p13.

Row 23: K12, M1, k1, M1, sm, (k11, M1, k1, M1, sm) twice, k12 (55 sts).

Row 25: K12, M1, k3, M1, sm, (k11, M1, k3, M1, sm) twice, k12 (61 sts).

Row 27: K12, M1, k5, M1, sm, (k11, M1, k5, M1, sm) twice, k12 (67 sts).

Row 28: P12, (sm, p3, cast on 4 sts in next st and cast them off immediately, p14) twice, sm, p3, cast on 4 sts and cast them off immediately, p15.

Row 29: K12, ssk, k3, k2tog, sm, (k11, ssk, k3, k2tog, sm) twice, k12 (61 sts).

Row 31: K12, ssk, k1, k2tog, sm, (k11, ssk, k1, k2tog, sm) twice, k12 (55 sts).

Row 33: K12, s1, k2tog, psso, sm, (k11, s1, k2tog, psso, sm) twice, k12 (49 sts).

Rep rows 10–22 once more.

Dec over the next few rows as follows:

Row 1: K6, (ssk, k4, M1, k1, M1, sm, k5) three times, ssk, k5 (51 sts).

Row 2 and alt rows unless specified: Purl.

Row 3: K6, (ssk, k3, M1, k3, M1, sm, k5) three times, ssk, k4 (53 sts).

Row 5: K6, (ssk, k2, M1, k5, M1, sm, k5) three times, ssk, k3 (55 sts).

Row 6: P9, (sm, p3, cast on 4 sts in the next st and cast them off immediately, p11) twice, sm, p3, cast on 4 sts in the next st and cast them off immediately, p12.

Row 7: K9 (ssk, k3, k2tog, sm, k8) twice, ssk, k3, k2tog, sm, k9 (49 sts).

Row 9: K9 (ssk, k1, k2tog, sm, k8) twice, ssk, k1, k2tog, sm, k9 (43 sts).

Row 11: K9 (sl 1, k1, psso, sm, k8) twice, sl 1, k1, psso, sm, k9 (37 sts).

Short row shape the top of the conker case as follows:

Row 12: P31, W&T leaving the last 5 sts on the left-hand needle.

Row 13: Sl wrapped st, k25, W&T.

Row 14: Sl wrapped st, p20, W&T.

Row 15: Sl wrapped st, k15, W&T.

Row 16: Sl wrapped st, p10, W&T.

Row 17: Sl wrapped st, k5, W&T.

Row 18: P to end of row.

Row 19: K to end of row.

Row 20: Knit (to form fold).

Change to B and work in rev st st, short row shaping as follows:

Row 1: Purl.

Row 2: K31, W&T.

Row 3: Sl wrapped st, p25, W&T.

Row 4: Sl wrapped st, k20, W&T.

Row 5: Sl wrapped st, p15, W&T.

Row 6: Sl wrapped st, k10, W&T.

Row 7: Sl wrapped st, p5, W&T.

Row 8: K to end of row.

Row 9: P to end of row.

Cast off.

Conker

Using 3.5mm needles and C, cast on 3 sts.

Row 1: Inc, k1, inc (5 sts).

Row 2 and alt rows unless specified: Purl.

Row 3: Inc, k3, inc (7 sts).

Row 5: Inc, k5, inc (9 sts).

Cont in this manner until 21 sts rem.

Work in st st without shaping for 13 rows.

Dec 1 st at the end of each foll row until 3 sts rem.

Cast off.

Lining (make 2)

Using 3.5mm needles and D, cast on 49 sts.

Work 23 rows in st st.

Dec as follows:

Row 24: K3, k2tog, (k8, k2tog) four times, k4 (44 sts).

Row 25: Purl.

Row 26: Knit.

Row 27: Purl.

Row 28: K3, k2tog, (k7, k2tog) four times, k3 (39 sts).

Row 29: Purl.

Row 30: Knit.

Row 31: Purl.

Row 32: K3, k2tog, (k6, k2tog) four times, k2 (34 sts).

Row 33: Purl.

Row 34: Knit.

Row 35: Purl.

Row 36: K3, k2tog, (k5, k2tog) four times, k1 (29 sts).

Beg with a purl row, work 7 rows in st st.

Cast off 2 sts at the start of the next 4 rows (21 sts).

Cast off.

Making up

Fold the white section to the inside of the case and stitch in place. Join the side seams of the conker case, leaving holes for the teapot handle and spout. Sew the conker to the inside of the top white section of the case, using the photograph as a guide.

Join the lining to the bottom of the conker case and join the side seams, leaving holes for the teapot handle and spout.

Join the lining to the case around the holes in the side seams.

Weave in all ends.

Nothing could look more charming on the tea table than a cupcake-inspired tea cozy. Quick and easy to make, this pattern would makes a perfect wedding present or a gift for a cupcake fan.

Cupcake

Materials

Rico Design Essentials Soft Merino Aran, 100% merino wool (109yds/100m per 50g ball)

1 x 50g ball in 059 Brown (A)

1 x 50g ball in 012 Orchid (B)

Small amount of 008 Red (C)

Small amount of 047 Fir Green (D)

4mm (UK8:USG/6) crochet hook

3.5mm (UK9:USE/4) crochet hook

Approx 30 white seed beads

Small amount of polyester toy stuffing

Dressmaking pins

1 x ½in (1.25cm) button

Sewing thread in co-ordinating colour

Tapestry needle

Tension

20 sts and 13 rows to 4in (10cm) over htr blo using 4mm hook. Use a larger or smaller hook if necessary to obtain the correct tension.

Special abbreviations

MC: Magic circle (see page 148)

Cupcake base

Row 1: Using 4mm hook and A, make 26ch.

Row 2: 1htr in 3rd ch from hook, htr into each ch to end, turn (24 sts). Work all sts now blo to create rib effect.

Rows 3–22: 2ch, 1htr blo into each st to end, turn (24 sts).

Row 23: 2ch, 1htr blo into next 6 sts, turn (6 sts).

Row 24: 2ch, 6htr blo, turn (6 sts).

Row 25: 2ch, 6htr blo, 14ch, then sl st in last 4 sts of row 22, turn (24 sts).

Row 26: 2ch, 1htr in 4 sl sts blo and then 1htr in each ch st, 1htr blo in 6 sts of previous row, turn (24 sts).

Rows 27–46: 2ch, 1htr blo into each st to end, turn (24 sts).

Without breaking off yarn, you will now work along the top of the cozy to create the picot edging. Work 2 picot points between each rib.

Picot edge: 3ch, sl st at base of chain, *1dc in next st, 3ch, sl st into where last dc was made; rep from * to end. Fasten off and weave in ends.

Cupcake icing

Round 1: With 4mm hook and B make a MC, work 6dc, sl st in first dc to join (6 sts).

Now work in continuous rounds.

Round 2: 2dc into each st (12 sts).

Round 3: (1dc, work 2dc into next st); rep around (18 sts).

Round 4: (2dc, work 2dc into next st); rep around (24 sts).

Round 5: (3dc, work 2dc into next st); rep around (30 sts).

Round 6: (4dc, work 2dc into next st); rep around (36 sts).

Round 7: (5dc, work 2dc into next st); rep around (42 sts).

Round 8: (6dc, work 2dc into next st); rep around (48 sts).

Round 9: (7dc, work 2dc into next st); rep around (54 sts).

Round 10: (8dc, work 2dc into next st); rep around (60 sts).

Round 11: (9dc, work 2dc into next st); rep around (66 sts).

Round 12: (10dc, work 2dc into next st); rep around (72 sts).

Round 13: (11dc, work 2dc into next st); rep around (78 sts).

Round 14: (12dc, work 2dc into next st); rep around (84 sts).

Round 15: (13dc, work 2dc into next st); rep around (90 sts).

Fasten off and weave in ends.

Strawberry

Round 1: With 3.5mm hook and C make a MC, work 4dc (4 sts).

Now work in continuous rounds.

Round 2: (1dc, work 2dc into next st); rep around (6 sts).

Round 3: (2dc, work 2dc into next st); rep around (8 sts).

Round 4: (3dc, work 2dc into next st); rep around (10 sts).

Round 5: 1dc in each st.

Round 6: (3dc, dc2tog); rep around (8 sts).

Round 7: (Dc2tog); rep around (4 sts).

Stuff the centre of the strawberry with a little polyester toy stuffing. Thread yarn through rem sts and pull up. Fasten off. Take a small amount of yarn D and, using a tapestry needle, embroider a basic five-pointed star at the end of the strawberry. Sew firmly to the top of the tea cozy.

Buttonhole

Using 3.5mm hook and A, rejoin yarn to the edge of the left side of the cupcake where the cozy opens for the handle, 5ch, miss 2 sts, sl st into next st, turn, work 7dc into ch loop, sl st at base of chain. Fasten off and weave in ends.

Making up

The WS of the cupcake icing should be uppermost. Pin the outside of the cupcake icing to the top of the tea cozy base.

Whip stitch (see page 150) the circumference of the cupcake icing to the inside of the brown tea cozy sides. Turn the tea cozy the right way round. With some co-ordinating sewing thread, sew the seed beads to the top of the cupcake in a random pattern.

Sew the strawberry firmly to the top of the tea cozy.

Using A, sew the top four stitches together at the top of the handle opening.

Sew a button on the right-hand side of the cozy to correspond to the buttonhole.

A naked teapot!

Techniques

Getting started

Tension

Tension is important, as just a slight difference can have a noticeable effect on the size of the finished cozy. If you are a new knitter or crocheter, it is a good idea to establish a habit that will save a lot of time in the end: work a swatch using the chosen yarn and needles or hook. These swatches can be labelled and filed for future reference. The tension required is given at the beginning of each pattern.

Working a swatch

To work a tension swatch, cast on or make a foundation row at least 24 stitches using your chosen yarn and needles or hook. Work for about 30 rows until you have produced a piece that is roughly square, then cast off or tie off. Press lightly, following the instructions on the ball band. Lay the swatch flat and measure carefully across the central section to check that your stitch count matches that of the pattern.

Materials and equipment

Needles and hooks

Most of the knitted designs in this book are worked back and forth on standard knitting needles. Bamboo needles are useful if you are using a rough-textured yarn as they are very smooth and will help to prevent snags. Some designs also call for double-pointed needles to make I-cord (see p. 151). For the crochet designs, the standard metal hooks that are widely available will be suitable, although bamboo hooks are also available if you prefer these.

Yarn

Cozies may be made in a huge variety of yarns. Wool or wool-mix yarns have the best insulating properties, but cotton or silk are also good. If you are using acrylic yarn, you may prefer to choose one of the thicker designs, or one that has a lining. Cozies are also an ideal way to use up oddments of yarn.

Substituting yarn

It is relatively simple to substitute the yarns recommended for the projects in this book if it is difficult to source or you have something in your stash that you would like to use. One way to do this is to work out how many wraps per inch (wpi) the yarn produces (see table). It is important to check your tension first. Then wind the yarn closely, in a single layer, around a rule or similar object, and count how many 'wraps' it produces to an inch (2.5cm). For a successful result, choose a yarn that produces twice, or slightly more than twice, the number of wraps per inch as there are stitches per inch in the tension swatch.

Tension required	Number of wraps per inch produced by yarn
8 sts per in (4-ply/fingering)	16–18 wpi
6.5 sts per in (DK/sport)	13–14 wpi
5.5 sts per in (chunky/worsted)	11–12 wpi

Knitting techniques

Simple cast-on

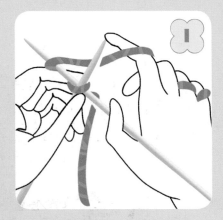

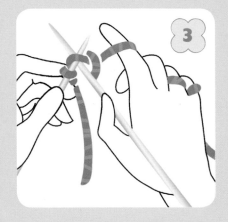

1 Form a slip knot on the left-hand needle. Insert the right-hand needle into the loop and wrap the yarn round it as shown.

2 Pull the yarn through the first loop to create a new one.

3 Slide it onto the left-hand needle. There are now two stitches on the left-hand needle. Continue until you have the required number of stitches.

Cable cast-on

For a firmer edge, cast on the first two stitches as shown above. When casting on the third and subsequent stitches, insert the needle between the cast-on stitches on the left needle, wrap the yarn round and pull through to create a loop. Slide the loop onto the left needle. Repeat to end.

Thumb method cast-on

1 Make a slip knot some way from the end of the yarn and place on the needle. Pull the knot tight.

2 Hold the needle in your right hand and wrap the loose tail end round the left thumb, from front to back. Push the needle point through the thumb loop from front to back. Wind the ball end of the yarn round the needle from left to right.

3 Pull the loop through the thumb loop, then remove your thumb. Gently pull the new loop tight using the tail yarn. Repeat until the desired number of stitches are on the needle.

Casting off

1 Knit two stitches onto the right-hand needle, then slip the first stitch over the second and let it drop off the needle (one stitch remains).

2 Knit another stitch so you have two stitches on the right hand needle again. Repeat this process until only one stitch remains on the left-hand needle. Break the yarn and thread through the remaining stitch.

Knit stitch

1 Hold the needle with the cast-on stitches in your left hand. Place the tip of the right needle into the first stitch and wrap the yarn round.

2 Pull the yarn through to create a new loop.

3 Slip the newly made stitch onto the right needle. Continue in the same way for each stitch on the left-hand needle.

Purl stitch

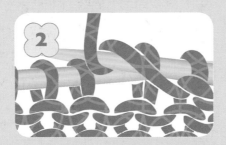

1 Hold the yarn at the front of the work as shown.

2 Place the right needle into the first stitch from front to back. Wrap yarn around needle anti-clockwise.

3 Bring the needle back through the stitch and pull through.

Cable stitch

With the help of a cable needle, these decorative stitches are quite straightforward to make. Stitches are slipped onto the needle and then knitted later to create the twists.

Front cable worked over 4 sts (cab4f)

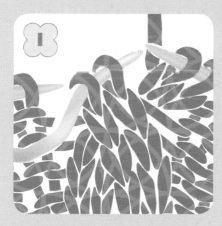

1 Slip the next two stitches onto a cable needle and hold in front of work.

2 Knit the next two stitches from the left needle as normal, then knit the two stitches from the cable needle.

Back cable worked over 4 sts (cab4b)

Slip the next two stitches onto a cable needle and hold at back of work.

Knit the next two stitches from the left needle as normal, then knit the two stitches from the cable needle.

1 Garter stitch

Knit every row.

2 Stocking stitch

Knit on right-side rows and purl on wrong-side rows.

3 Reverse stocking stitch

Reverse stocking stitch is the same as stocking stitch, but start with a row of purl stitches followed by a row of knit stitches. The purl side forms the right side of the work.

4 Single rib

With an even number of stitches:

Row 1: *K1, p1* rep to end.

Repeat for each row.

With an odd number of stitches:

Row 1: *K1, p1, rep from * to last st, k1.

Row 2: *P1, k1, rep from * to last st, p1.

5 Double rib

Row 1: *K2, p2, rep from * to end.

Repeat for each row.

Carrying yarn up work

When you return to the beginning of the knit row after working a row of purl, pass the working yarn under the yarns not being used at the edge of the work. Knit the next row. Repeat these two rows. The unused yarns will sit in a nice twist at the side edge of your work. When needed, they will be sitting at the beginning of the next knit row.

Picking up stitches

To pick up stitches along a cast-on or cast-off edge, working from the right side of the fabric, hold yarn to back of knitted fabric. Insert needle through the opening of the 'V' of the stitch in the row just below the cast-on edge, wrap yarn around needle as if to knit and pull a loop through onto needle.

To pick up stitches along the side, you will generally pick up stitches in 3 out of 4 rows. With right side facing, insert needle between two bars, one stitch from the edge.

Advanced techniques

Fairisle

Fairisle knitting uses the stranding technique of colourwork, which involves picking up and dropping yarns as needed. The different yarns are then carried across the row. Loops are formed along the back of the work; these should not exceed about five stitches in length or they will start to tangle. Make sure the loops are of even tension, or your fabric may pucker.

1 Start knitting with the first colour (A), which is dropped when you need to incorporate the second colour (B). To pick up A again, bring under B and knit the next stitch with A.

2 To pick up B again, drop A, bring B over A and knit the next stitch with B.

Reading charts

In this book, charts are used for intarsia and Fairisle designs. Charts are shown in squares, with each square representing one stitch. They are usually marked in sections of ten stitches, which makes counting easier. When working in stocking stitch on straight needles, read the chart from right to left on knit (RS) rows and from left to right on purl (WS) rows. Check carefully after every purl row to make sure the pattern stitches are in the right position.

Intarsia

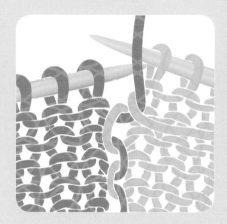

Blocks of colour are created by using the intarsia technique of twisting the yarns at the back of the work with each colour change (see diagram above). It is better to wind a small amount of yarn onto bobbins, rather than using whole balls, to prevent tangling. The bobbins are smaller and easier to handle and can hang at the back of the work out of the way. Once the work is finished, the ends are woven in at the back and pressed carefully under a damp cloth to help neaten any distorted stitches.

Felting

Sew in any yarn ends carefully before starting the felting process. Place the items to be felted in a net bag, washing bag or pillowcase and put it in the drum of a washing machine. Add a bath towel or a pair of jeans to provide the friction necessary for felting. Add a small quantity of washing powder and run through one full cycle at 100°F (40°C). Remove the felted items and check that they have felted sufficiently. Pull gently into required shape and leave to dry naturally.

Felting will reduce the size of a knitted item by up to one-third. If the work does not felt sufficiently on one cycle, you can repeat the process. If items seem too small after felting, ease gently to make them bigger. Remember that perfect results can be guaranteed only when using natural, untreated wool yarn. 'Superwash' treated wool will not felt, and wool blends may not felt. It is advisable to test a sample square of your chosen yarn before felting a finished item.

Crochet techniques

Chain stitch (ch)

1 With hook in right hand and yarn resting over middle finger of left hand, pull yarn taut. Take hook under then over yarn.

2 Pull the hook and yarn through the loop while holding slip knot steady. Repeat to form a foundation row of chain stitch.

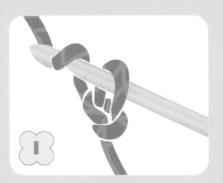

Slip stitch (sl st)

1 Slip the hook under the top two strands of the 'V' of the first stitch of the row.

2 Wrap yarn around hook and draw it back through both the 'V' and the loop on the hook.

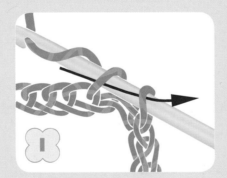

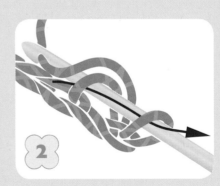

Double crochet (dc)

1 Start by placing hook into a stitch. Wrap new yarn round the hook and draw loop back through work towards you. There should now be two loops on the hook.

2 Wrap the yarn around hook once more, then draw through both loops. There should now be one loop left on the hook. One double crochet stitch is now complete. Repeat as required.

Half treble (htr)

1 Wrap yarn around hook and place into a stitch. Wrap yarn around hook and then draw the loop through. There should now be three loops on the hook.

2 Wrap yarn around hook again and draw through the three loops. There should be one loop left on the hook.

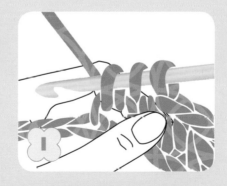

Treble crochet (tr)

Follow instructions for half treble until there are three loops on the hook.

1 Catch the yarn with hook and draw through two of the loops.

2 Catch yarn again and draw it through the remaining two loops.

Double treble (dtr)

Follow instructions for half treble until there are three loops on the hook.

1 Wrap yarn around hook twice and then place into a stitch.

2 Wrap yarn around hook and then draw the loop through (four loops should now be on hook).

3 Catch the yarn and draw through two of the loops.

4 Catch yarn again and draw it through two loops.

5 Catch the yarn once more and draw through the remaining two loops.

Magic circle

Use a magic circle to make a very tight centre.

1 Make a half-formed slip knot.

2 Make all the first-round stitches into the circle.

3 Pull the end tight after completing one round.

Finishing off

Sewing up seams

Stocking-stitch joins

When joining stocking-stitch pieces, use mattress stitch for an invisible seam and a neat finish. After pressing, place the pieces side by side with right sides facing. Starting at the bottom, secure the yarn and bring the needle up between the first and second stitch on one piece. Find the corresponding point on the other piece and insert the needle there. Keep the sewing-up yarn loose as you work up the seam, then pull tight.

Garter-stitch joins

It is easier to join garter stitch as it has a firm edge and lies flat. Place the edges of the work together, right side up, and see where the stitches line up. Pick up the bottom loops of the stitches on one side of the work and the top loops of the stitches on the other side. After a few stitches, pull gently on the yarn. The stitches should lock together and lie completely flat. The inside of the join should look the same as the outside.

Slip stitch

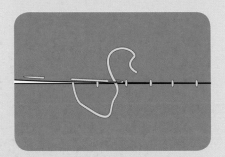

This stitch is used to join two folded edges or to fasten a lining inside a knitted project. Fasten the thread and working from right to left bring the needle up through one folded edge and then back through the other peiece of fabric to make a tiny stitch. Contnue along the row, running the thread between the fold so that it doesn't show.

Whip stitch

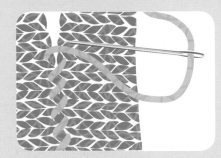

1 Start with the right sides of your pieces facing and the edges to be seamed together. Use matching yarn for an invisible seam. Insert the sewing needle from the right side through the first edge stitch on the right-hand piece and through the first stitch on the left-hand piece from the wrong side.

2 Pull the yarn through. Carry the yarn over the top of the work and insert needle into next stitch on each piece in the same way.

3 Repeat this process, taking up one stitch from each edge with each stitch.

Backstitch

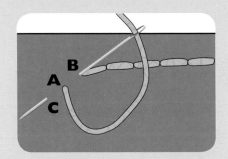

Make a knot to secure yarn at back of work. Bring the needle up to point A, insert at point B, and bring back up at point C. Repeat, keeping the stitches an even length.

Finishing touches

Making a pompom

1 Cut out two cardboard circles a little smaller in diameter than the pompom you want. Make a hole in the middle of both about a third of the diameter. Place both circles together and thread lengths of yarn through the central hole, wrapping evenly round the outer edge until the card is completely covered. Use one or more colours for different effects. Continue working in this way until the centre hole is only a pinprick.

2 With sharp scissors, cut all around the edge of the circle, slicing through all the strands of yarn.

3 Now ease a length of yarn between the card discs and tie very firmly around the centre, leaving a tail for sewing. You have now secured all the strands of yarn around the middle. Ease the card discs away from the pompom and fluff out all the strands. Trim any loose or straggly ends.

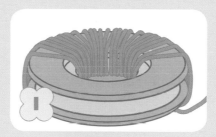

Making an I-cord

Using two double-pointed needles, cast on the required number of stitches – typically five (fewer stitches will give you a narrower cord). Do not turn the work. Slide the stitches to the opposite end of the needle, then take the yarn firmly across the back of work. Knit the stitches again. Repeat until the cord is the desired length. Cast off, or follow instructions in pattern. An I-cord may be grafted to stitches left on a needle after working another part of the pattern.

Embroidery stitches

Blanket stitch

Work from left to right. The twisted edge should lie on the outer edge of the fabric to form a raised line. Bring needle up at point **A**, down at **B** and up at **C** with thread looped under the needle. Pull through. Take care to tighten the stitches equally. Repeat to the right. Fasten the last loop by taking a small stitch along the lower line.

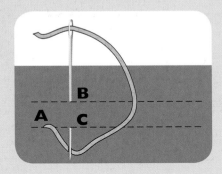

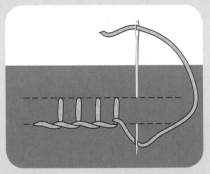

Cross stitch

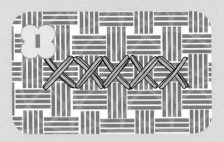

1 Start from the top left of the stitch, then bring the needle through from the bottom, holding the tail at the back of the thread.

2 Bring the thread down to the lower right corner.

3 Take it back up through the upper right and down through the lower left, forming an X. Each time you should pull the thread all the way through so that it is flush with the fabric surface.

4 Start your next stitch so it uses two of the same holes as the first one.

French knots

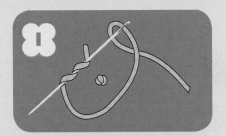

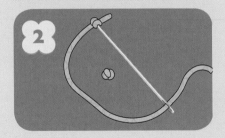

Work in any direction.

1 Bring needle to RS of fabric. Holding thread taut with finger and thumb of left hand, wind thread once or twice around needle tip.

2 Still holding thread, insert needle tip close to the point where you brought the needle out to the RS of work and pull needle to back so that the twist lies neatly on the fabric surface. Repeat as required.

Abbreviations

alt	alternate
approx	approximately
beg	beginning
blo	back loop only
cab4b	cable over four stitches holding two stitches at back of work
cab4f	cable over four stitches holding two stitches at front of work
ch	chain stitch
ch sp	chain space
cm	centimetre(s)
cont	continue
dc	double crochet
dec	decrease
dpn(s)	double-pointed needle(s)
foll	following
g	gram(s)
g st	garter stitch
htr	half treble
in	inch(es)
inc	knit into front and back of stitch
k	knit
k2tog	knit two stitches together
k2tog tbl	knit two stitches together through the back loop
k3tog	knit three stitches together
k-wise	knit-wise

m	metre(s)
M1	make stitch by picking up strand of yarn that runs between stitch just worked and next stitch on LH needle
M1L	insert left-hand needle, from front to back, under strand of yarn that runs between stitch just worked and next stitch on the left-hand needle. Knit this stitch through the back loop
M1R	insert left-hand needle, from back to front, under strand of yarn that runs between stitch just worked and next stitch on the left-hand needle. Knit this stitch through the front loop
MB	make bobble
MC	magic circle
mm	millimetre(s)
p	purl
p2tog	purl two stitches together
p3tog	purl three stitches together
patt	pattern
PB	place bead
pm	place marker
psso	pass the slipped stitch over
p-wise	purl-wise
rem	remain(ing)
rep	repeat
rev st st	reverse stocking stitch

RS	right side
skpo	slip one stitch, knit one stitch, pass the slipped stitch over
sl	slip
sl2, k1, p2sso	slip two stitches, knit one stitch, then pass both slipped stitches over the knit stitch
sm	slip marker
sl st	slip stitch
sp	space
ssk	slip two stitches knitwise; knit these two stitches together through the back of the loops
st st	stocking stitch
st(s)	stitch(es)
tbl	through back of loop
tog	together
tr	treble
tr2tog	treble two stitches together
W&T	wrap and turn
WS	wrong side
wyf	with yarn in front
yb	yarn back
yds	yards
yf	yarn forward
*	work instructions following *, then repeat as directed
( )	repeat instructions inside brackets as directed

Conversions

Knitting needle sizes

UK	Metric	US
14	2mm	0
13	2.25mm	1
12	2.5mm	–
–	2.75mm	2
11	3mm	–
10	3.25mm	3
9	3.5mm	4
9	3.75mm	5
8	4mm	6
7	4.5mm	7
6	5mm	8
5	5.5mm	9
4	6mm	10
3	6.5mm	10.5
2	7mm	10.5
1	7.5mm	11
0	8mm	11
00	9mm	13
000	10mm	15

Crochet hook sizes

UK	Metric	US
14	2mm	B/1
12	2.5mm	C/2
11	3mm	–
10	3.25mm	D/3
9	3.5mm	E/4
8	4mm	G/6
7	4.5mm	7

UK/US yarn weights

UK	US
2-ply	Lace
3-ply	Fingering
4-ply	Sport
Double knitting	Light worsted
Aran	Fisherman/worsted
Chunky	Bulky
Super chunky	Extra bulky

UK/US crochet terms

UK	US
Double crochet	Single crochet
Half treble	Half double crochet
Treble	Double crochet
Double treble	Triple crochet

List of authors

Susan Ainslie: Big top (p. 110)

Sian Brown: Harlequin (p. 18); Love hearts (p. 42); Nordic (p. 64); Pansies (p. 106); Rose garden (p. 90)

Elaine Bryan: Country garden (p. 22)

Janet Crinion: Get well soon (p. 68)

Charmaine Fletcher: Monet (p. 46)

Ally Howard: All buttoned up (p. 30); Colourful cables (p. 82); Elegant entrelac (p. 56); Felted diamonds (p. 114); Gerbera (p. 14); Jester lovely cuppa (p. 98); With love (p. 10)

Rachel Proudman: Bonkers conker (p. 126)

Lynda Shilton: Bobble madness (p. 94)

Nicola Valiji: Tea and bunting (p. 76)

Emma Varnam: Cross stitch (p. 60); Cupcake (p. 130); Owl (p. 38); Plum pudding (p. 86); Pumpkin (p. 118); Granny squares (p. 102), Pretty pompom (p. 72); Shell-pattern stripes (p. 34)

Woolly Mamma (Gayle Foster): Black poppy (p. 26); Tea roses (p. 52); Vintage roses (p. 122)

Index

To place an order, or to request a catalogue, contact:

GMC Publications Ltd

Castle Place, 166 High Street, Lewes, East Sussex, BN7 1XU

United Kingdom

Tel: +44 (0)1273 488005

Website: www.gmcbooks.com